THE TOP 20 RIVALRIES

IN THE PAST 20 YEARS

SHOWDOWNS

THE TOP 20 RIVALRIES
IN THE PAST 20 YEARS

JEREMY ROBERTS

pocket books

new york toronto sydney london

CONTENTS

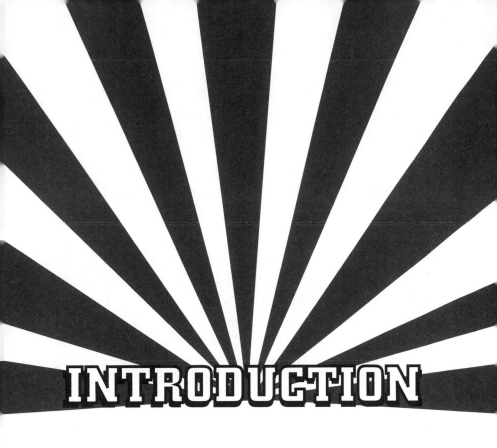

INTRODUCTION

WHAT MAKES A SHOWDOWN?

Ask anyone why he or she likes pro wrestling, and the answer is easy—the matches.

But a good wrestling match is only part of a longer story. Without something at stake, two guys or two gals clawing at each other is of only passing interest. Without something at stake, fans have no reason to care about the outcome of a match. Yes, many fans admire Rey Mysterio's athleticism or Triple H's moves; they are astonished that Ric Flair can still give it up after all these years or that Batista can move so gracefully despite his size. But for most of us to *really* care who wins, we need a conflict, a dispute of some kind. We may not see every match as a clash between good and evil, but we still want it to be a fight between someone we care about and someone we hate, if only for that match.

To use a word many wrestling purists hate: we need a feud.

IN THE BEGINNING, GOTCH & HACKENSCHMIDT

Stories have always been an important part of pro wrestling, even in the days before television. Back in 1908, thousands of fans flocked to Dexter Park Pavilion in Chicago to see the showdown between George Hackenschmidt, aka the Russian Lion, and Frank Gotch. It was a fight between Old Europe (Hackenschmidt) and the American Midwest. It was a battle between old wrestling and new. But most deliciously of all, it was a conflict with skullduggery, conspiracy, and a good dose of controversy.

Gotch was born and bred in Iowa, and in many ways he was an almost perfect candidate to be an all-American sports hero. Good-looking—always a plus—he was considered one of the era's best athletes, on a par with the best boxers and baseball players. His fighting weight was listed at just over two hundred pounds, with his height at five eleven. There's a good chance those numbers aren't exact, but who's to argue now? Contemporary pictures show a well-muscled but not tremendously tall man with very large biceps and core muscles a bodybuilder would die for.

His opponent, Hackenschmidt, was born in Estonia, at the time part of the Russian Empire. History books claim he was about five nine and wrestled at two ten; based on photos of the match with Gotch, he seems to have been both shorter and heavier. Both men were born in 1878 and were in the prime of their careers when they clashed.

Greco-Roman wrestling, the sort we see today at the Olympics, was still the accepted traditional form. While Hackenschmidt had gone well beyond the traditions—among other things, he's credited with inventing the bear hug as a wrestling move—he'd made a name for himself early on by winning a score of Greco-Roman-style matches in Europe. Americans therefore saw him as the old style's standard-bearer.

Gotch, on the other hand, was a wrestling wild man, the era's Mick Foley. His fame came from catch-as-catch-can or freestyle wrestling, a new invention at the time. Competitors could grab any part of an opponent's body and use it to bring him to submission. The match ended only with a pin—two shoulders against the mat—or a submission. Today's freestyle, as practiced in American high schools and colleges as well as by amateur wrestling associations throughout the country, is a direct descendant of catch-as-catch-can, with more formal rules developed over the years.

SKULLDUGGERY

The run-up to the Gotch-Hackenschmidt match would be familiar to any contemporary fan, with standard appeals to nationality and the promise of a tough fight. Hackenschmidt, who'd already defeated the reigning American wrestling champion, was heavily favored.

The match, though, was something else. The controversy it generated and the mists of time make it difficult to know precisely what happened in the ring, but it seems pretty clear that Gotch used all manner of shady techniques to give himself the advantage. For sure, he oiled his body, making it hard for Hackenschmidt to grab hold of him. He gouged and scratched his opponent and purposely fouled to change the rhythm of the match and gain a break.

Standard operating procedure these days, but scandalous (at least to the press) back then.

Whatever the truth, Gotch and Hackenschmidt wrestled for an incredible two hours, grabbing, punching, and generally rasslin' back and forth. At two hours and three minutes — a curiously specific number that appears in several accounts — the match was called by the referee.

Why?

Hackenschmidt quit. To this day, it's not clear whether he gave up because of a very painful ankle hold Gotch applied, or because he simply had grown so frustrated at Gotch's style of mayhem that he couldn't take it anymore.

The match was no sooner over than Hackenschmidt began telling reporters and anyone else who'd listen that he'd been robbed. Gotch had cheated, he said, oiling his body and pulling countless illegal moves. He was a no-good so-and-so and worse. And his dog wasn't much better.

The press ate it up.

The controversy generated so much heat that a rematch was natural. It was eventually scheduled for Chicago's Comiskey Park in 1911. But before the meet could take place, Hackenschmidt got hurt.

That appears not to have been a coincidence. It's generally believed that Gotch hired someone to injure Hackenschmidt during a training session. The practice was a new twist on an old carny trick. In the early days, wrestlers were part of the traveling carnival and would take on local amateurs for prize money. A "hooker" would take out a particularly adept local wrestler, ensuring a victory (and the purse) for the promotion's employee.

The injury was to Hackenschmidt's right knee. He'd been hospitalized for a similar injury in 1904, a fact that some sources take as confirmation that a plot was involved.

Whether or not the injury was intentionally caused, Hackenschmidt wanted to call off the bout. Gotch, who knew they were both up for a big payday, came up with his own injury. Saying he'd hurt his neck, Gotch implied that he was just as wounded as Hackenschmidt, so what was the big deal?

The money involved made a deal inevitable. The two men—and the promoters—supposedly worked out an arrangement allowing Hackenschmidt to win one of the three falls that would determine the bout; Gotch would take the other two and get the victory.

If Gotch agreed to carry Hackenschmidt, he forgot all about it as soon as the match began. Upwards of thirty thousand people saw him quickly get the better of his opponent, two falls to none.

Soon after, the news media reported on the deal, dirty in itself, and the subsequent (alleged) double cross. There was a fury—and, predictably, great interest in a rematch.

Alas, Hackenschmidt's injuries convinced him to retire. Gotch wrestled for another two years, reigning as World Heavyweight Champion until 1913, when he officially retired.

ALL THE ELEMENTS

Even though it took place a hundred years ago, the Gotch-Hackenschmidt showdown was remarkably modern in outline. Fans might start out backing a national hero, the presumed good guy, only to discover that he was really the bad guy and switch their allegiance. Double crosses, cheating, backroom intrigue—all fodder for next week's *Raw or SmackDown!*

Of course, there was one more critical ingredient: The wrestling itself was superb, at least in the first match. If only for its length, unusual even at the time, the first Gotch-Hackenschmidt fight is still considered one of the all-time great wrestling events.

MODERN SHOWDOWNS

While Gotch and Hackenschmidt's rivalry may have been the prototype, much has been added as pro wrestling evolved. The advent of television, and then cable and Pay-Per-View, not only added more memorable matches but made it necessary for wrestlers to expand their story lines. Because they were playing to the same audience week after week, they needed new wrinkles to keep things interesting.

Then came the time of the Monday Night Wars, a hothouse period of development in sports entertainment. World Wrestling Entertainment (better known as WWE) and Turner-owned World Championship Wrestling (WCW) not only presented viewers with more prime-time wrestling than ever before, they changed the nature of the story lines and, by extension, wrestling itself.

Seeking to find a way to get an advantage over its competition, WCW under Eric Bischoff made wrestlers' personal lives part of the show. Nothing was too real or too personal to be part of the plot. And *nothing* was sacred. To give just one of a score of examples: Arn Anderson, a fan favorite and one of the true all-time greats, was famously mocked and satirized during and after his on-air retirement by the heel faction New World Order (or nWo, as it was styled). The controversy generated was very real—many people thought nWo and Bischoff went *way* too far—and the heat was incredible as Arn's allies sought revenge.

Good for the ratings, though.

That was nothing compared to the video attacks staged by D-Generation X, WWE's answer to the New World Order. Shot documentary-style, on location and in the field, the bits directly challenged the rival wrestling organization. They tried to get into their headquarters building and into their events, then aired the results. It was reality TV years before the concept became popular.

At the time, of course, the two companies were separate, and there was no way they were going to work together on a joint contest. So the controversy played out only as a shouting match, much to the disappointment of many fans.

MORE THAN A "FEUD"

Why do so many people — Vince McMahon, the reigning genius of the sport, included — hate the word "feud" when it's used to describe a story line conflict?

The truth is, the word fails to capture the full nature of what fans are caught up in. A feud is something small, something limited to grievances, generally arising in a specific time and place. Great wrestling story lines have that, but they also have much more. Stone Cold didn't *just* disrespect The Rock; the conflict between them went much farther.

They represented different approaches to wrestling and reflected cultural differences. Never mind that they might use the same moves in the ring, or admire the other's ability.

Still, "feud" does suggest one important facet of the story lines that has intrigued fans over the years: Something personal has to be at stake for the match to get our blood pulsing.

Maybe it starts with name-calling. Maybe it's a heck of a

lot more personal than that—a girlfriend stolen, a car trashed. Heels are known for being sneaky, and as a rule make the first dirty move, but once the gauntlet is thrown, a response is demanded. Getting even sometimes means crossing the line. Soon, all sorts of lines are being crossed.

How do you know if a particular story line has real heat?

If a wrestler walks into the arena and you immediately start looking, hoping, even demanding that his opponent appear. That's a story line with heat.

If the clash is truly great, you don't feel excitement when the first wrestler walks toward the ring—you get scared. You don't know what will happen next, but you know it will be ruthless, violent, and maybe even disgusting. And you know, even if you're up in the nosebleed section, there's a very good possibility that you'll be going home with blood on your clothes.

Hopefully not your own.

THE CRITERIA

Choosing the best of anything can be a difficult task. When it comes to wrestling, though, it's nearly impossible. No one person can give a definitive list of anything. Too much depends on personal preferences—does a fan like athletic wrestling or prefer brute force, for example. Even with all the advantages the Internet brings, it's impossible for anyone to see or have seen every meet.

Still, it's fun to try.

When the idea for this book was first proposed, the publisher and WWE assembled a blue-ribbon panel of fifty wrestling experts to evaluate the story lines and make recommendations. They gathered for several months, working long into the night as they debated which story lines to nominate.

By March 2008, they had largely finished their selection and were preparing to hand over their work. They gathered for a final planning session in an undisclosed location. As luck would have it, it was the night of *WrestleMania XXIV*, and naturally they gathered around several large-screen TVs to watch the show in the middle of their work.

Then the unimaginable happened. An electrical malfunction short-circuited the screens in the room where they were gathered. A fire ensued. The experts escaped, but their extensive notes were largely destroyed.

For reasons best left unstated, I inherited the project along with the bar tab. With the help of a forensic scientist, I assembled the tattered records and organized them into the book that follows.

The experts had started with a set of simple criteria:

- Only twenty showdowns could be chosen. This was so they could fit in a single book.
- Only showdowns from the mid-1990s onward were eligible to be considered. They seem to have fudged this one as well.
- To be considered, a showdown had to include a series of matches and play out over an extended period of time. Although a single match might be more memorable than others, the rivalry should not be summarized by any one particular show.
- Finally, the showdown should have generated *more* than one hall of fame match, though that rule was suspended in one instance.

I took on the job hoping to be able to consult with one or more of the experts; I had many questions about their opinions, selective memories, and above all their deliberations. (I was especially intrigued by the bar tab, which indicated that at least one prominent wrestling expert drinks absinthe, a liquor I can't even spell.) Alas, they had scattered to the winds, and no amount of searching turned them up. So I did the best I could and take only passing responsibility for the choices.

HISTORY

Looking at these showdowns is in many respects a meditation on the recent history of sports entertainment. From Hogan to Batista, from Flair to Mysterio, the rivalries reveal the trends in wrestling's unique form of storytelling. Interestingly, recent trends seem to be a bit old school, where outlandish stories and characters take a backseat to the show in the ring. But perhaps that's just the perspective gained from looking at select snapshots.

In salvaging the notes about these stories, I had limited space—though, in truth, I went far over my allotment, managing to get it extended only with pleas, threats, and blackmail. Some of the feuds are so well known that they could be covered with fewer words than the others. Some seemed to provoke the verbosity gene inherent in all writers. Thus, readers should remember that the length of the narratives is *not* a reflection of the interest the story line generated or its importance or entertainment value.

With only a few exceptions, the story lines fit within much larger and more complicated arcs. Most—say, the so-called alliance/invasion angle with WCW and ECW challenging

WWE for dominance—are both well known to hard-core fans and irrelevant to the individual story lines, so I felt no obligation to discuss them except in cases where that was necessary to illuminate the conflict between the individual wrestlers. Frankly, the stories are so intricate that in many cases any attempt to neatly summarize them misses the point.

Longtime fans are probably already screaming at the injustice done to their favorite rivalries, and to sports entertainment itself. Undoubtedly, they can name half a dozen better feuds from the same time period.

The author is a jerk, a dweeb, an uneducated @#$@#$, and worse. And his dog isn't much better.

To that I say: *Bring it on, suckbrains.*

With any luck, we'll all be back for a rematch . . . and this time, you're paying.

HULK HOGAN VS. RANDY SAVAGE

The 1980s were a golden era for wrestling, though few realized it at the time. Thanks largely to World Wrestling Federation, wrestling not only became a national entertainment phenomenon but also gained cultural significance transcending the sport. This was the rock star era, when one of the biggest pop stars of the moment—Cyndi Lauper—joined with wrestling greats to reach a mass audience inconceivable to earlier generations of wrestling fanatics.

And the man at the center of the ring for most of this era was Hulk Hogan.

HULKAMANIA

Like the Great Depression and Woodstock, *Hulkamania* was an event you had to live through to completely understand. Made possible by the ascendance of World Wrestling Federation, it was very much a product of its time and place.

Today, it's not uncommon to see entire movies built

around a prominent wrestler. But in the 1980s, Hogan's appearances as a star in movies and TV were radical developments. That exposure, along with the *WrestleMania* extravaganzas featuring stars from other entertainment fields, brought new audiences to wrestling.

Hulkamania was much more than Hulk Hogan and his fans. But as the most visible wrestler of his time, Hogan not only leant his name to the phenomenon, he popularized and symbolized a certain type of wrestling. Big men, big muscles, over-the-top story lines, heels as popular as good guys—all existed before Hulk Hogan. But none were mainstays of the industry until Hogan. Google some wrestling stars from the 1950s or '60s or '70s if you need to be convinced.

HOGAN

Hogan began wrestling professionally in 1977 when he was twenty-four. His peak years began with his return to World Wrestling Federation in 1983 and lasted until 1993. After that, he joined WCW, helping to transform it from a struggling operation to (briefly) the number-one wrestling franchise in the world. After WCW's collapse, he returned to WWE as popular as ever.

He continues to enjoy a successful career in the public eye as an entertainer and (often bedeviled) reality TV star; his name is synonymous with wrestling even today.

Hogan's opponents are a *Who's Who* of great wrestlers. Hogan had memorable encounters with everyone from Nick Bockwinkel to the Iron Sheik to Roddy Piper, Andre the Giant, Ric Flair, Sting, and The Rock. Picking one or two story lines from his long career is like trying to determine which grain of sand on the beach is better than the others.

Some of his most memorable confrontations at the height of his fame came with Randy Savage, and their long and slightly twisted feud was as entertaining as any.

RANDY SAVAGE

"Macho Man" Randy Savage joined World Wrestling Federation in 1985. Almost immediately, he became one of the top heels in the promotion. Somewhat pompous and full of himself, Savage was managed by Miss Elizabeth, soon to be a star in her own right.

Before meeting Hogan in 1987, he had several great matches, the best of which was the epic encounter with Ricky Steamboat at *WrestleMania III*. Late in 1987, toward the end of a feud with the Honky Tonk Man, Savage found himself outnumbered in the ring by a group of wrestlers that included the Hart Foundation. Miss Elizabeth managed to get Hulk Hogan to help bail Savage out. A new alliance was formed among the three, who called themselves the Mega Powers.

Some sexual tension was evident to fans, as the beautiful Miss Elizabeth seemed to sparkle not only for Savage but for Hogan as well. The sexual innuendos added a tantalizing element to the rivalry.

WRESTLEMANIA IV

At *WrestleMania IV*, Hogan helped Savage win the title from Ted DiBiase by hitting him with a chair. The friendship between Hogan and Savage continued after the match; wrestling as the tag team Mega Powers, they dominated their opponents over the next year or so. Then jealousy over Miss Elizabeth ended the alliance.

At the *Saturday Night's Main Event* in February 1989,

Savage accidentally knocked Miss Elizabeth out during a Tag Team match against the Twin Towers. With Savage busy in the ring, Hogan picked up Miss Elizabeth and carried her into the dressing room for medical attention. This left Savage to take the brunt of the Towers' onslaught.

Savage wasn't particularly pleased when Hogan returned, and he gave his partner a taste of his own medicine, declining to intervene when the Towers had Hogan on the ropes. Hogan received a substantial beating before managing to finish off the Towers on his own.

The match was over, but the rift between the two friends had just begun. Savage attacked Hogan following the match, and it was soon clear that the dispute had more to do with Hogan's attentions toward Miss Elizabeth than with what had happened in the ring.

Bad blood boiled. Hogan challenged Savage to a championship showdown. Savage accepted. The tension built, right up to *WrestleMania* V (April 2, 1989).

Then Savage got hurt. An arm injury led to a swollen bursa sac at his elbow. When this got infected, his entire arm swelled up. Days before the match, Savage was in bed with a serious fever and blood poisoning, in no shape to compete.

Not that he was willing to admit that.

"Don't worry about the Macho Man," Savage told friends. "I'll be there."

WRESTLEMANIA V

Savage showed up at Trump Plaza in Atlantic City with a wrap on his right elbow big enough to preserve a well-fed mummy. The infection had been drained, but he was still suffering the effects of the ailment. No matter. He and Hogan went out and tussled in one of the great matches of both men's storied careers.

Taller than Savage by several inches, Hogan chased him from the ring soon after the bell. Buff and in his prime, Hogan nonetheless had a hard time keeping up with Savage as the smaller man literally ran him around the ring. Savage had little reason to stop—whenever he got close enough, Hogan used his superior size to great advantage, either by giving him a closed-fist jab or overpowering him in a hold.

Savage absorbed an enormous beating in the middle of the match but kept getting up for more. Flinging his body across the narrow confines of the ring again and again, he rallied the crowd. They seemed grudging at first, but gradually the cheers grew louder and louder.

Miss Elizabeth saved Savage at one point, then kept things balanced by nursing Hogan while he was out of the ring. Savage reacted strongly, pushing her out of the arena before returning to attack Hogan.

A cut opened over Hogan's left eye, negating Hogan's size advantage. Savage moved in for the kill. Hogan countered with a monstrous kickout that sent Savage high into the air.

Hogan began to get his adrenaline as the crowd became frenetic. A tremendous flurry of slaps, punches, a kick and legdrop—Savage was pinned, momentarily unconscious.

A tremendous roar went up. The champion had reclaimed what was rightfully his.

THE FIGHT CONTINUES

The Savage-Hogan feud continued for a few months, fueled by sexual and professional jealousy. Both wrestlers formed new partnerships for a tag team showdown. Savage dumped Miss Elizabeth for a new manager—Sensational Sherri—and partnered with Zeus.

Not to be outdone, Hogan called on Brutus "The Barber" Beefcake to man his corner. Miss Elizabeth also made a cameo to support him.

Before a filled Meadowlands Arena in East Rutherford, New Jersey, Hogan and The Barber prevailed over Savage and Zeus. The match was the end of a story that had run well over a year, but it was not the final time in their history that the two would face off.

WCW

Hogan went to WCW in 1994, becoming the focus of the franchise the moment he signed his contract. Savage followed, just in time for *Starcade*, the promotion's late December Pay-Per-View.

There was a great deal of speculation about whether Savage would be Hogan's friend or enemy. At the event, he saved Hogan from a pile-on by the 3 Faces of Fear, one of whom was the Butcher. Hogan defeated Butcher to keep the Championship belt, and he and Savage were friends again. For a while, at least.

Savage feuded with Ric Flair, reprising their earlier clashes in the World Wrestling Federation. He teamed with Hogan at *Clash of the Champions XXX*, where they beat Kevin Sullivan and the Butcher, and was generally his ally.

Then came 1996 and the New World Order (nWo). Joining the stable of very cool heels, Hulk Hogan became Savage's archenemy.

Savage, now representing the traditional WCW, feuded

ferociously with Hogan and his cohorts week after week. At *Halloween Havoc* in 1996, he and Hogan faced off in a fight where Miss Elizabeth was once again a main motivator.

Though older, Savage still displayed his trademark athleticism. As Hogan strutted in his sunglasses and golden wig—he'd "gone Hollywood"—Savage ran, raining blows on his old adversary. Hogan staggered, helpless as Savage stole his glasses and wig.

The crowd roared in delight.

Hogan finally dropped his mugging. Picking up a chair, he knocked Savage senseless during an exchange outside the ring.

Miss Elizabeth couldn't decide who to help. She loved Savage, but Hogan had offered to make her a film star. She went back and forth for a while, distracting both wrestlers and teasing the crowd with peeks at her charms.

Then the match became a Free-For-All. The ref was knocked out. Hogan was knocked out. Savage decided to chase Ted DiBiase around for kicks. The Giant appeared, grabbed Savage, and chokeslammed him into unconsciousness.

The match ended with The Giant carrying Savage into the ring, where he placed Hogan's arm over him for the countout.

MORE NWO

After the match, Savage disappeared for several months. When he came back in January 1998, he was Hogan's friend, aiding him against Roddy Piper with the timely pass of a pair of brass knuckles.

Over the course of the next year, Hogan and Savage

remained allies. But anyone who knew their history realized the arrangement was fragile.

Hogan, sensing that Savage was a threat to the leadership of nWo, tried to sabotage him at *Spring Stampede 1998*, where Savage fought Sting for the championship. Savage won, setting up a grudge match the next night with Hogan on *Nitro*, WCW's prime-time TV show.

NITRO SHOWDOWN

The *Nitro* match turned out to be one of their best. Despite their age, Hogan and Savage flung themselves around with abandon.

Hogan repeatedly slapped Savage's face, jawing for the camera as he pushed Savage against a turnbuckle and demanded, "Who's head of the nWo? Who? Who?"

Savage had severely injured his knee and wore a brace for the match. The knee took a ferocious beating through the first ten minutes or so of the contest, as Hogan and his sidekick the Disciple battered the knee again and again.

With the crowd chanting his name, Savage rallied. He managed to throw Hogan over his shoulder, dazing him. Savage climbed the ropes and dove on Hogan, nearly covering for the pin.

Hogan rebounded. He put Savage into a figure-four (a leglock that applies tremendous pressure to the knees) and threatened to break his leg. Summoning all of his strength, Savage crawled to the ropes and won a reprieve. He regained his momentum if not his footing; hopping on one knee, he managed a finger-choke on Hogan.

But just as it looked as if Hogan would pass out, the Disciple jumped into the ring. The match became a donnybrook. The ref was knocked out. Savage went down as well. Hogan and the Disciple dragged him to the ring post and took turns slamming his injured knee against it.

Kevin Nash ran in to stop the beating. Eric Bischoff tried grabbing Nash, who promptly threw him off and flattened the Disciple. Nash then gave a jackknife to Hogan and put the prostrate Savage on Hogan. Bret Hart ran in, nailed Nash, rearranged the bodies, and dragged the ref over to demand he count out Savage. The ref complied. Chaos ensued.

THE END

The Hogan-Savage *Nitro* match marked the splitting of nWo into rival factions. It was also the end of one phase of Savage's career, as he needed to take time off for surgery on his knees. When he returned roughly a year later, it was clear he was going to face off against Hogan as soon as possible.

Savage won the WCW championship at *Bash at the Beach* in July 1999, using an array of underhanded tactics to defeat Kevin Nash. (This was actually a Four-Way Team match, with Savage and Sid Vicious teaming up against Nash and Sting; the first man to get a pin or submission got the title, which was held by Nash.)

Hogan challenged Savage after the win; the two went at it on *Nitro* the following night.

Savage—heavier than in their first match and with his once untamed hair slicked back and tied in a ponytail— dominated the early going. Hogan rallied. When Madusa and Mona tried to interfere, Hogan clinked their heads together and sent them packing. Then he began pummeling Savage. Hogan bent a chair over Savage's head, then bashed him into an announcer's table.

Savage managed to get his breath back and climbed in-side the ring. Regaining his footing, he rallied and took con-trol of the match. Even so, the audience chanted Hogan's name. Savage grabbed a strap. He whipped Hogan unmerci-fully, until finally Hogan could stand no more. Jumping from the canvas, Hogan unleashed a fury of punches on Savage that ended only when Savage kneed him in the groin.

That just made Hogan angrier. He turned to the crowd and began hulking up—the same tactic he'd used in his early years. The fans loved it.

Hogan decked Savage, then turned to the audience. He held his hand to his ear.

What do you want me to do? he asked wordlessly.

"Finish him!" they shouted.

He held his hand to his ear again.

I can't hear you.

The fans roared louder.

But before Hogan could turn Savage into tiny human bread crumbs, the ring action was interrupted by Sid Vicious, who interfered on Savage's behalf. Sting jumped to Hogan's defense, pounding Vicious and pulling him out of the ring— but not before Vicious passed off a chain to Savage.

Swinging his chain, Savage took Hogan down. But before he could get a pin, Kevin Nash came in and laid him flat, revenge for his stealing the bout the night before. With Sav-age stunned, Hogan crawled over and got an easy pin.

It was the last time the two titans faced each other in the ring.

A LONG RUN

The Hogan-Savage showdown ran the whole arc from *Hulkamania* to the Monday Night Wars and the dawn of The Attitude Era of wrestling. Sex, outside distractions, run-ins, and other mayhem characterized their encounters over the years.

At its heart, though, the story was simple: two champions fighting for the title and the attention of a pretty girl. It was a conflict every fan could identify with, which is why it was so memorable.

MR. PERFECT
VS. RIC FLAIR

Wrestling is an art of strength, skill, and emotion. On any given night, anything can happen. Injuries, feedback from the crowd, even the vagaries of diet and family life distractions can all subtly influence the outcome of a match. The best a wrestler can hope for over a long career is some kind of consistency, prevailing more often than not.

Only one wrestler has ever been "simply perfect." Wrestling to him was not an art but a science—or so he claimed.

That wrestler was Curt Hennig, known as Mr. Perfect during his World Wrestling Federation career. And perhaps it was fitting that his most memorable stint in the company came when he was paired with, and then up against, a man whose career was a model not just of consistency but of consistent triumph: Ric Flair.

MR. PERFECT

Like many successful wrestlers, Curt Hennig came from a wrestling family. His father, Larry "The Ax" Hennig, was a star with Verne Gagne's American Wrestling Association. But it wasn't until he was injured playing football at the University of Minnesota that Curt became interested in his father's profession. Looking to rehab his injury, he went to Verne's wrestling camp and fell in the love with the sport. He made his professional debut in 1979 when he was twenty-one, starting a career that would stretch right up to his death in 2003.

In 1988, Hennig joined World Wrestling Federation, which had become the dominant franchise in sports entertainment. (He also wrestled there briefly in the early 1980s.) Hennig bragged to owner Vince McMahon that he was perfect in every sport he tried. McMahon called him "Mr. Perfect," and the name stuck. And he was perfect. A series of videos showed Hennig competing against various popular sports stars, such as Wade Boggs, at the time the best hitter in baseball. Mr. Perfect beat them all. He excelled at whatever he tried. He sank a three-hundred-foot putt, bowled a perfect game, sank a free throw behind his back—he was always perfect.

He wasn't bad at wrestling either. He reeled off a winning streak in the ring that extended through confrontations with the Blue Blazer, the Red Rooster, and Jimmy Snuka. Only Hulk Hogan was good enough to beat him consistently, and only then after epic matches.

And then came Ric Flair.

THE BUILDUP

Flair and Mr. Perfect first hooked up outside of the ring, while Hennig was working off an injury. Mr. Perfect became

Flair's executive consultant, joining financial adviser Bobby Heenan as Flair mounted a challenge for the World Wrestling Federation title at the end of 1991 into 1992.

Flair took the championship at *Royal Rumble* in January 1992, holding out in the match for an incredible fifty-nine minutes. (In a rumble, wrestlers enter the ring at intervals, their entrance spots drawn at random. The last wrestler left standing wins. In general, the later you enter—or the higher your number—the better your odds of winning. Flair drew number three in the match.)

Flair lost his title to Randy Savage at *WrestleMania VIII*, Savage gaining revenge after Flair claimed that he and Savage's manager (Miss Elizabeth) had been lovers. The pair faced off for several more months, with Flair aided by several allies, including Mr. Perfect. Finally in September, Flair regained the title, thanks in part to a diversion by Mr. Perfect that helped him bamboozle his way to victory.

BACK IN ACTION

While all of this was going on in front of the cameras, behind the scenes Mr. Perfect was getting back in shape to reenter the ring. Savage, noting this, asked Mr. Perfect to partner with him in a Tag Team match against Flair and Razor Ramon planned for *Survivor Series*, the annual tag team event held each November.

Mr. Perfect just laughed. No way he was fighting against his friend Ric Flair. Then Bobby Heenan, Flair's other adviser, commented on air that Mr. Perfect was washed up.

Hmmmmmm.

Mr. Perfect angrily changed his mind and agreed to hook up with Savage. That led to a quick spat between Heenan and Mr. Perfect, who caught the commentator completely off guard, humiliating him on air. (The exchange was aired on *Prime Time Wrestling* and ranks as one of the show's highlights.)

Mr. Perfect and Savage beat Flair and Razor Ramon. Flair didn't like the fact that his consultant had turned against him. The two men were locked on a path toward mutual destruction.

Mr. Perfect tangled with Flair at the *Royal Rumble 1993*, causing his disqualification and upping the ante on their personal animosity.

THE MATCH

Their showdown came the next night on *Raw*. Since it was clear the company was too small for both of them, it was decided the loser would leave.

The contest began with some face slapping back and forth, as well as some bad-mouthing at the ropes. A Flair tumble livened things up, and the two men began showing they could move quickly and gracefully despite their size. In one memorable exchange, they literally flew by each other, trading throws as well as blows. Perfect knocked Flair to the canvas and even managed to get his butt into his face. He couldn't get the pin, though.

"Perfect! Perfect!" chanted the crowd. But it was Flair who took the advantage. He got Mr. Perfect in a headlock, losing his grip only after Perfect crashed into the turnbuckle. Flair then worked into a figure-four leglock and, aided by an illegal hold on the rope, threatened to break Mr. Perfect's limbs.

When the move failed, Flair grew desperate. Thrown toward the ropes, he pulled a "foreign object"—a set of brass knuckles—from his sock and used them to lay Perfect out. Though he recovered in time to prevent a pin, Perfect began to bleed, and within moments his face was a bloody mess.

The pain seemed to transform him. Now he wasn't the man whose every movement was textbook perfect. No more was he a mechanical strongman, a wrestler who hit his marks with scientific precision. Now he was angry, now there was emotion in his moves, not perfection.

And emotion trumps all.

In a rage, he leaped across the ring, attacking Flair with new fury. The crowd chanted. The clock spun down toward the end of the show. Mr. Perfect got his pin—and Flair was kicked out of World Wrestling Federation.

BRET HART VS. STEVE AUSTIN

Stone Cold Steve Austin arrived at World Wrestling Federation in 1995 after a stint at WCW. He was a respected wrestler but not well known by the fans—until he faced Jake "The Snake" Roberts.

Roberts liked to quote scriptures, usually using them to predict or celebrate his triumph in the ring. After defeating him in the match, Stone Cold proclaimed one of his own:

> *You sit there and you thump your Bible and say your prayers, and it didn't get you anywhere! Talk about your psalms, talk about John 3:16. . . . Austin 3:16 says, I've just whipped your ass.*

Before too long, signs with the inscription "Austin 3:16" turned up everywhere, not only at wrestling matches but in the stands at other sporting events as well. Austin was well on his way to becoming a wrestling legend.

BRET HART

Austin's basic approach to wrestling was in-your-face nasty. He was a mean ol' junkyard dog, a rattlesnake come to tear your head off, accepting no shit from anyone. He used power and intimidation to dominate his opponents.

Bret Hart's approach was more involved, almost scientific in its way. "The Hitman" emphasized what he called "the excellence of execution."

A popular star long before Austin arrived, he'd made his first bones wrestling as one half of the tag team The Hart Foundation and won his first Intercontinental Championship in a match against Mr. Perfect at *SummerSlam 1991*.

In 1996, Hart left wrestling for a while to pursue a career as a movie actor. Nearly forty, with a long run at the top of his profession, Hart could hardly have been blamed for retiring. But he didn't. Instead, after an eight-month absence, he signed an unprecedented twenty-year contract with the World Wrestling Federation and prepared to make his return.

It was a decision that put him on a collision course with Austin.

THE MATCHES

The feud between Austin and Bret Hart began during the summer of 1996, even before Hart got back into the ring. Austin began calling him out at different events, saying he would take him on, taunting him on air as a quitter and worse.

Hart finally took Austin's challenge, coming back to the ring at *Survivor Series*.

"The excellence of execution," said Austin sarcastically during the promo before the match. "Bret, clichés are clichés . . . and you're gonna get an ass whippin'."

As things turned out, it was Stone Cold's words that didn't quite match his deeds. The Rattlesnake's key Million Dollar Dream move not only failed to put Hart out; Hart was able to reverse it and claim the victory.

The contest kicked off a rivalry that changed wrestling.

WRESTLEMANIA 13

They met each other in a series of matches that extended from *Survivor Series 1996* through *Royal Rumble 1997*, *In Your House 13*, and finally *WrestleMania 13*. Along the way there were a number of memorable *Raw* matches.

The *WrestleMania* match is, unarguably, the high point and culmination of the confrontation. It remains an all-time hall of fame contest, in many ways typical not just of their showdowns but also the era.

Stone Cold and the Hitman got right at it, jumping on top of each other and quickly carrying their conflict out of the ring. With no disqualifications, and no win except by submission, the wrestlers spent nearly five minutes dragging, pushing, and pummeling each other through the audience, reaching the bleachers before eventually being urged back to the ring by guest referee Ken Shamrock.

Back between the ropes, Hart attacked Stone Cold's knee, only recently healed from an injury. Hart tied Austin into a figure four against the steel post of the ring's ropes. Despite the pain, Austin refused to submit and eventually freed himself.

CROWD ON HIS SIDE

Somewhere around the middle of the match, Austin began bleeding during an exchange on the ring apron. Back inside the ropes, Hart tried a Sharpshooter, his finishing move, but Austin escaped.

The crowd roared.

In their first match, Austin had a good contingent of followers, but Hart was clearly the fan favorite. Now the crowd's allegiance was reversed. Austin was applauded wildly for nearly everything he did; Hart's backers were much more subdued.

Blood covering his face, Austin unleashed a fury of kicks while Hart was backed up against the ropes. A suplex put Hart down, allowing Austin to jump outside and grab an electrical cord. Before Stone Cold could choke him into unconsciousness, Hart managed to grab the timekeeper's bell. He flung it wildly, fighting out of the hold.

A punishing exchange followed, with Hart finally putting Austin into the Sharpshooter. Austin refused to submit, bringing the crowd to its feet with the chant, "Austin! Austin!"

"Submit?" asked the ref.

Austin refused.

The ref asked again.

No.

Submit?

Never.

Austin passed out from the pain, or from oxygen being cut off to his brain (depending on which narrative you prefer), and Hart got the victory. Then, to cement his turn back to heel, Hart attacked not only Austin but also the ref. Walking away from the ref without accepting his offer to fight, Hart received a shower of boos from the crowd.

It didn't matter. The match, and the epic struggles preceding it, had cemented Stone Cold Steve Austin's status as the most popular wrestler of The Attitude Era.

NWO
VS. D-GENERATION X

Can a story line that never actually resulted in a head-to-head match be considered truly great?

It can if it involved the Monday Night Wars and two of the greatest heel factions in the recent history of the sport, nWo and D-Generation X.

WCW'S RISE

Younger fans will have hard time believing this, but WWE has not *always* dominated pro wrestling. For a brief period of time in the mid- and late 1990s, WCW not only challenged it for leadership but actually pulled higher ratings for its television and Pay-Per-View events.

World Championship Wrestling was pulled together by Ted Turner from the NWA or National Wrestling Alliance in 1988. After several years of misstarts, personnel changes brought Eric Bischoff to the fore as the company's leading executive. Bischoff, after successfully luring Hulk Hogan to the franchise, took WCW on a rapid ride, first to credibility and then profitability. By 1995, Ted Turner was sufficiently confident of Bischoff and the company to "suggest" that WCW go head-to-head against the World Wrestling Federation's *Raw* TV show with a live Monday night show of its own.

Turner owned the network, and any suggestion he made was essentially an edict. Bischoff and company came up with the idea for *Monday Night Nitro* literally within hours, and it was only a matter of weeks before they went on the air.

The tone of competition between the two franchises was set on the very first *Monday Night Nitro* in September 1995. Lex Luger jumped from World Wrestling Federation and appeared on the program. *Nitro* and *Raw* were in each other's face from that moment on.

Aired live (at the time, about half of the *Raw* shows were taped), *Nitro* was far edgier than *Raw* and much more willing to be controversial. WCW also initiated a number of innovations, highlighting cruiserweight competitions, for example, bringing a more athletic style of wrestling to prime time.

The backing of the Turner Broadcast Network (and later Time Warner, which Turner became part of) gave WCW the deep pockets necessary to establish itself in the marketplace. Still, *Raw* generally outscored it, until 1996, when the New World Order dawned.

NWO

New World Order was part story line, part heel stable. It evolved out of an unusual confluence of events. The origin itself was relatively simple: Scott Hall and Kevin Nash, two popular wrestlers, came over to WCW in the spring of 1996. Looking for a way to introduce them, Bischoff hit on the idea of having them play the role of outsiders "invading" the promotion.

It was a radical notion—star newcomers had always been announced and welcomed with great fanfare—but the idea made sense on many levels. The wrestlers *were* outsiders, at least to the established *Nitro* order. More important, Bischoff saw it as a way to break down the wall between audience and wrestlers, getting fans to suspend their disbelief and put themselves wholly into the story and match.

Still, the New World Order (or the Outsiders, as they were first called; the name New World Order and the logo nWo came later) wouldn't have worked without excellent performers.

Bischoff found them in Hall and Nash. They added an edgy, trouble-around-the-corner feel to the proceedings. Both came to WCW with strong followings—Hall as Razor Ramon and Nash as Diesel. The fact that they had to leave behind their character names and wrestle as "themselves" played right into Bischoff's blurring of reality and fiction.

Hall, Nash, and those who joined them operated like a street gang intent on busting up a corporation. After being dubbed the New World Order, they adopted a logo that looked as if it was spray-painted graffiti. But what really made the showdown popular was the defection of Hulk Hogan, who turned heel at *Bash at the Beach* in July 1996, joining the Outsiders in one of the great turns of all time.

Fans were so angry that they filled the ring with garbage. He delivered a speech that riled them even more, attacking the audience in a way few wrestlers had ever dared.

"The first thing you have to realize, brother," he shouted, "is that this is a new world order. This is the future of wrestling. . . . You fans can stick it, brother. If it wasn't for Hulk Hogan, you people wouldn't be here."

The fans' reaction was visceral and deeply emotional. At many shows, tempers boiled over and the wrestlers legitimately feared for their lives.

THE TRIUMPH OF BAD-BOY "COOL"

Then a funny thing happened—the nWo became cool. Nash and Hall were so hip, so rebellious, that they became popular antiheroes, just like many movie stars and musicians. They were the Hell's Angels, Butch Cassidy and the Sundance Kid, and a thousand street corner rappers all rolled into one ever-expanding wrestling faction.

Over the course of the next year, nWo dominated WCW, taking *Nitro* to the top of the ratings. The showdown also brought a cinema verité feel to the show, making it appear as if it were real life, not an act (today we would call it reality TV). As Eric Bischoff wrote in his book, *Controversy Creates Cash*, it turned wrestling inside out.

WCW matches in this period relied heavily on run-ins and interference by various allies of the wrestlers in the ring. An enormous number of bouts ended in disqualifications and general mayhem.

FIGHTING BACK

World Wrestling Federation fought back. While Stone Cold Steve Austin and his famous confrontations with Mr. McMahon deserve most of the credit for returning the franchise to its traditionally dominant position, it was the heel faction

D-Generation X and the stories connected with it that took the battle directly to the rival promotion.

Literally.

Debuting in September 1997 as a morph of the Clique, D-Generation X (or DX as it came to be styled) was a heel faction led by Shawn Michaels and Hunter Hearst-Helmsley, better known now as Triple H. With the slogan "Suck it" and their trademark crotch chops, they were role models of degeneration, the antiheroes as crude teenage loudmouths.

Again, they may have been heels, but they were definitely cool. Every teenage boy—and quite a few older men and women—secretly wished he too could tell his boss, his workmates, his enemies to "Suck it." Inspired by DX, they probably did.

THE DX ARMY

The name D-Generation X was a play on Generation X, a popular reference to the era's twenty-somethings. Following the baby boom generation, they were criticized as slackers and worse. The DX story line turned the put-down into a rallying cry.

As wrestlers, the members of DX were more over-achievers than slackers. Triple H took over as the leader of the faction following injuries to Shawn Michaels. He immediately became one of the greatest Superstars of the modern era.

THE INVASION

Both WCW and World Wrestling Federation sniped at each other on the air. Bischoff gave away the results of *Raw* matches that had been pretaped; McMahon introduced a character that satirized Ted Turner. But it was the DX army that brought the battle directly to the enemy.

In the spring of 1998, with the story line peaking, the DX faithful organized into an army. They dressed in fatigues, borrowed a jeep, and went in search of their opponents at WCW.

Literally.

The DX army showed up at WCW events and at its head-quarters, calling out the company and its wrestlers. The bits were then aired on television.

On April 27, 1998, DX members attempted to disrupt the WCW *Nitro* show in Norfolk, Virginia. Though they didn't actually enter the arena, their antics were incorporated into the *Raw* show, to the great pleasure of *Raw* partisans. For several weeks following, *Nitro* prepared to deal with a more successful invasion by DX into its performances, though none was ever made.

Many fans were rooting for a real confrontation between the two companies and their wrestlers. In fact, Bischoff challenged McMahon to a wrestling match and even made contingency plans to cover what to do if he showed up. Unfortunately, cooler heads prevailed, and there never was a real confrontation.

"ASSES IN THE SEATS"

The Monday Night Wars peaked in mid-1998 as the two shows traded places in the Nielsen ratings. *Nitro* steadily slipped as the year went on, pushed downward by the wildly successful feud between Stone Cold Steve Austin and Mr. McMahon.

World Wrestling Federation had been slow to play WCW's

game, but once it embraced "attitude," it did it with a vengeance. Meanwhile, WCW's story lines had become a bit stale. Corporate decisions would soon take their own toll on the organization.

The closing phase of the Monday Night Wars began with an ill-advised attempt on January 4, 1999, to ruin the ending of a rival *Raw* match. Announcer Tony Schiavone told viewers that former WCW wrestler Mick Foley—now wrestling as Mankind—was going to win the championship title on *Raw*. A good portion of *Nitro*'s audience changed stations. Schiavone's sarcastic quip about Mankind taking the championship—"That'll put asses in the seats"—became a rallying cry for *Raw* fans.

It was the beginning of the end. Before the year was out, Bischoff had been sent home and WCW was in disarray.

It's hard for younger fans to realize the impact of the Monday Night Wars on wrestling, or how radical The Attitude Era seemed when it began. It was a time of turmoil and change, chaos and mayhem—and a golden era for wrestling, which thrives on all those things.

5

MANKIND
VS. SHAWN MICHAELS

There has never been a more bizarre Superstar than Mankind. An immediate sensation upon joining World Wrestling Federation in 1996, Mankind was what the Hunchback of Notre Dame might have been had he devoted himself to wrestling. He lived in a boiler room and regularly communed with a rat . . . and that was his normal side.

So imagine what it must have felt like to face him in the ring.

If you can do that, then you can feel Shawn Michaels's pain.

MANKIND

Mankind was man's bastard offspring, the doom of the world come to life and then pushed into a dark corner, from which he would rise to mutilate his progenitors. He wore a leather mask inspired by one worn by the serial killer and cannibal

Hannibal Lecter in the movie *Silence of the Lambs*. He perfected a move called the mandible claw: Shoving two fingers into his opponent's mouth, he struck a unique set of nerves for an inescapable if unorthodox finish. Sometimes he spoke in riddles. Sometimes he didn't speak at all. He was different. And definitely not in a good way.

"Of all the things I've lost in my life," he said in an early interview, "the thing I miss most is my mind."

Mankind took the fans by storm . . . and whatever other means were available. Within weeks of his introduction, he faced Undertaker in a high-profile Pay-Per-View match. Not too many weeks after that, he was angling toward a showdown with Shawn Michaels, the World Wrestling Federation Champion.

WITH MICHAELS

The showdown between Mankind and Michaels began on a September 6 *Raw* while Mankind was still feuding with Undertaker. Previously, Mankind had helped Goldust by spooking Michaels out of the ring. Though Michaels managed to return and defeat Goldust, the encounter unnerved him. He tried ducking questions about Mankind during an interview the next week on *Raw*, until at last he said it never made sense to hunt what you couldn't kill—probably the best advice for anyone dealing with Mankind.

Naturally, it was advice he couldn't follow. Michaels defeated Mankind on September 16 *Raw* in a quick match that set the stage for a much longer confrontation in Philadelphia at *In Your House: Mind Games*.

MIND GAMES

Mankind came to *Mind Games* in a casket, and rather than showing himself off to the crowd, he rocked in a corner of the ring as Paul Bearer looked on. (Paul Bearer was ordinarily Undertaker's sidekick, but he'd semiadopted Mankind after his arrival.) Mankind cradled an urn in his arms, worshiping it as if it held the key to the universe.

Michaels, jumping into the ring as fireworks exploded and his music pumped the refrain "I'm just a sexy boy," glanced occasionally at the bizarre creature cowering in the corner across from him. As the name of the Pay-Per-View suggested, Mankind was definitely in Michaels's head, and the champ looked tentative and even shaky at the start of the match. Mankind began with his typical brawling style, punching and kicking, using his size against Michaels. When the action shifted outside the ring, Mankind lifted one of the apron mats, trying to expose the concrete and make the brawl that much more brutal. But when Michaels launched a flying dropkick, it was his head that hit the ground.

"Mankind's head just bounced off the concrete floor," said one of the announcers, "and he probably enjoyed it."

Wary of the mandible claw, Michaels nonetheless dominated the first ten minutes or so of the match. A suplex onto the stairs took the starch out of Mankind's attack, and he began favoring his left leg. After a string of acrobatic moves by Michaels, Mankind started to rally. After throwing his opponent into the ropes, Mankind got a pen or a knife (it's not precisely clear which) from Paul Bearer and plunged it repeatedly into his injured leg. This odd therapy seemed to do the trick; not only did his leg no longer hurt him, he was able to use it to kick Michaels as the match turned around.

The crowd seemed stunned into silence, unsure what Mankind might do next. Battering Michaels with kicks and the occasional headbutt, Mankind threw him against the turnbuckle, leaving the wrestler draped there as he threw himself against his head.

Michaels escaped, setting up a sequence at the edge of the ring just outside of the ropes. At the end, Mankind was in a hangman. He escaped by threatening to unleash the mandible claw; Michaels released his hold rather than succumb to the voodoo death touch.

Back in the ring, Michaels went after Mankind's right hand, hoping that by stomping it he'd never have to face the mandible claw again. Mankind managed to flick Michaels over his back, sending him to the concrete outside. Now it was the monster's turn to dominate, punishing his opponent with a variety of hard smashes to every part of his body.

After a Mankind DDT failed to seal the pin, the two wrestlers put on a display of different moves and holds, each ending with a kickout at a two count. For a character not known for his technical expertise, Mankind did a more than plausible job and held his own. Michaels's in-ring storytelling, meanwhile, wove the audience into the ring, selling the battering he was taking as one of the more ferocious in his career.

Michaels got a burst of fear-driven adrenaline after Mankind tossed him into the casket he'd brought to the ring. Climbing the ropes, he launched himself at his opponent. Not to be outdone, Mankind grabbed him, and then from the turnbuckle launched himself backward onto a table outside the ring. The wrestlers crashed to the floor with a shockingly loud crunch.

It still wasn't over. Somehow, they managed to get back into the ring. Michaels tried for a pin; Mankind kicked out. Before either wrestler could regroup, Vader ran in and disrupted their match. Sycho Sid then came out, adding to the chaos.

Michaels was finally downed in the fracas. Mankind attempted to roll him off into the casket. Paul Bearer opened the lid—and out came Undertaker, who threw Mankind from the ring, bringing the match to a close.

Michaels won the bout by disqualification, and both wrestlers went on to continue different rivalries. The contrast in styles had produced a memorable, though often overlooked, showdown.

6

SHAWN MICHAELS
VS. BRET HART

Discussed in numerous books, articles, and wrestling websites, and even the focus of a documentary movie, the Montreal Screwjob is without a doubt one of wrestling's most controversial and best-known events. Coming at the height of the Monday Night Wars, it was for many symbolic of the lengths World Wrestling Federation and its head, Vince McMahon, would go to stay alive.

The controversy tended to obscure some of the context not only of the final match where the screwjob took place but also of the rivalry between Michaels and Hart that set the stage for it.

A HERO AND LEGEND

Younger American fans—and maybe American fans in general—will have a hard time understanding the controversy if they don't realize that Bret Hart was considered a genuine hero to many Canadians. Not a *wrestling* hero, not a *sports* hero, but an outsized pop culture phenomenon. There were many reasons for this, including his success in America. His absence from the ring in the mid-1990s, when he briefly pursued an acting career, only made him more popular.

Hart also had had a long and close relationship with Vince McMahon, which added to the feelings of betrayal as events unfolded.

LONG HISTORY

Bret Hart and Shawn Michaels's history with World Wrestling Federation stretched back to 1992 when they faced off against each other in a series of matches that began right after *WrestleMania VIII*. Their confrontations culminated in a Ladder match in July 1992 at a house show in Portland, Maine. It's regarded as the company's first Ladder match, and it echoed a similar meet Hart had used when he was wrestling with Stampede Wrestling, his father's Canadian promotion, where he started his career.

When they started their feud, Hart was Intercontinental champ; Michaels was still a relatively new singles wrestler in World Wrestling Federation. In the months immediately afterward, Shawn Michaels became better known, gradually gaining the stature and skills to become a champion. According to Michaels, he and Hart were on good terms—not close but friendly—and remained so until 1996, when they met in a one-hour Iron Man No-Falls match for the World Wrestling Federation Championship at *WrestleMania XII*.

The rules of an Iron Man match give the victory to the wrestler with the most falls on his opponent during a specified time frame. In this case, neither wrestler got a single pin, and thus they went to sudden-death overtime after the marathon.

A PERSONAL THING

Whatever the status of their relationship before the match, afterward there was a noticeable cooling off. Hart, who wrote a newspaper column popular in Canada, criticized Michaels, then apologized. Michaels wasn't placated.

"This was a pattern with him that drove me nuts," said Michaels. "He would say things about me, apologize, and then go right out and say more bad things about me."

For his part, Michaels freely shared his opinion that Hart was a very good wrestler, but not great.

Behind the scenes, this was a difficult time for the company. The conflict with WCW was costly, and there were serious financial concerns. Many Superstars had jumped ship, and the promotion was struggling to find the right combination to win fans back. There was also resentment between different wrestlers who felt that a small group of performers around Michaels was being favored to the detriment of others.

BRET'S CONTRACT

Michaels held the title for much of the rest of the year. Hart, meanwhile, took time off from wrestling to act.

While he was out of the company, Hart was approached by WCW and offered a large contract. He turned them down. In the fall of 1996, he signed a new contract with World Wrestling Federation for twenty years, an unprecedented commitment, especially given the fact that he was approaching forty.

The contract also gave Hart "reasonable" creative control over his matches, including a say in how they ended.

Back with the company, Hart began working toward a confrontation with Michaels for the championship. His greatest feud in this period was with Steve Austin, who was rocketing to the top of the profession, but he had memorable confrontations with Sycho Sid and a number of other wrestlers as well.

All were intended to set the stage for the Michaels-Hart confrontation in 1997.

The showdown was delayed when an injury forced Michaels to give up the title. Hart did take the championship, however, setting up a showdown with the former champ Michaels, who was once more coming on as an arrogant (but successful) S.O.B. Hart also began an on-air rivalry with Mr. McMahon, who was working as an announcer and liked to punctuate his commentary with jabs at Hart and his legend.

Behind the scenes, Hart says he considered McMahon more a friend than an employer. The pair had a long relationship and, in Hart's mind at least, were close.

According to Hart, McMahon came to him in the fall of 1997 and said that the company was in deep financial trouble and would not be able to afford the new contract. McMahon, says Hart, urged him to talk to WCW.

It didn't take long for the rival franchise to work out an agreement with Hart. McMahon agreed to let Hart out of the contract, and according to Hart the two worked out an arrangement that would let Hart drop the title just before his "defection" to their rivals. Supposedly, Hart's major concern was that he not lose in Canada, his home turf, and McMahon agreed.

But either there was no agreement, or McMahon became concerned that Hart wouldn't keep his word. The company had been embarrassed by defections before, and as things played out, McMahon acted before it could happen again.

THE SCREWJOB

Bret Hart's decision to join the rival organization was not a well-kept secret, and when he showed up to wrestle Shawn Michaels at *Survivor Series* in Montreal on November 9, 1997, there were signs near the front row telling him to just leave now.

So much has been written about the controversy that marred the end of the match that the rest of the contest has been overshadowed. A little less than half as long as their Iron Man fight, the match featured some of Michaels's best wrestling.

Michaels, at this point part of the heel group DX, started riling the crowd even before Hart appeared, playing with a Canadian flag and mocking Hart's patriotism. His cocky, arrogant persona established, he attacked Hart as soon as the champion held up his championship belt.

For the next fifteen minutes, the two wrestlers attacked each other in a slugfest outside the ropes. The bell hadn't even rung, but they were ringing each other's, slamming themselves back and forth until four refs and McMahon managed to convince Hart to drag Michaels back from the entrance ramp and down to the ropes.

HOME CROWD FAVORITE

As you'd expect, the crowd was firmly behind Hart, even as Michaels began dominating. After Michaels had beaten Hart for more than five minutes, spearing him with a small wooden flagpole and punishing him with his fists, one fan near the front row jumped to his feet and shouted, "Irish wimp!" an epithet hung on Michaels by his opponents.

Hart brought the crowd to life with a figure four on the ring post that slowed Michaels, seemingly setting him up for the signature Sharpshooter close. But Michaels reversed it, sending Hart to the rope for a break.

Hart climbed the ropes and jumped in, trying to lay his opponent out. He missed his target, allowing Michaels to get him in a Sharpshooter—

Then the match ended, referee Earl Hebner claiming to hear a submission that Hart never uttered.

AFTERMATH

The premature ending to a match he was expecting would end in a disqualification (letting him hold the title a few days more) left Hart confused, angry, and embittered, in exactly that order. He stood in the ring a moment, staring down at McMahon before seeming to yell "bullshit" at him.

In the locker room a short time later, Hart bashed television equipment and then punched McMahon for good measure.

(While it has often been said that Michaels was as surprised as Hart—and he did look surprised at the match—he was clearly in on it. In his memoir he not only said that he knew but also admitted taking part in the planning and execution. He seems to have taken a lot of pleasure out of beating and "screwing" Hart, whom by then he disliked on a personal level.)

Reactions among the wrestlers were mixed. Wrestlers lose championship titles all the time, and a number, including Ric Flair, simply scratched their heads over Hart's emotion.

Others, like Mick Foley, were deeply offended that the outcome of the match had been changed and shocked by the way things were handled. (Foley, wrestling as Mankind at the time, briefly walked out in protest.)

The confrontation seemed to galvanize McMahon and World Wrestling Federation. Perhaps it was coincidental, but the company soon turned the corner against its rival.

Hart, on the other hand, never seemed to fully recover from the incident. Widely reported, the incident gained Hart a great deal of sympathy, much more than he might have gotten if viewed simply as a defector. He came to his new employer as a babyface rather than a heel. But his time in WCW was marked by contests a rung or two under the franchise's main attractions.

Shawn Michaels and his DX mate, Triple H, stayed on in World Wrestling Federation, helping it rebound in the Monday Night Wars while also shaping The Attitude Era. Michaels's career eventually overshadowed the Montreal Screwjob. Among other things, he won a great deal of respect following his successful recovery from back surgery in 1998, and has long been considered a legend in his own right.

7

UNDERTAKER VS. KANE

Hell hath no fury like Undertaker, the six-foot, ten-and-
a-half-inch Dead Man who has haunted WWE wrestling arenas since 1990. Perhaps best known for his
undefeated streak at *WrestleMania*, Undertaker has been
one of the most popular and dominating figures since his arrival on the scene.

But if one man could meet the soul destroyer on somewhat even terms, it was his brother, Kane.

And whatever your opinion on brotherly love, this series ap-
pealed to anyone who liked fire and lightning, and lots of it.

UNDERTAKER

Undertaker came to World Wrestling Federation in 1990 as
a member of Ted DiBiase's Million Dollar Team. First known
as Cain the Undertaker, his role in the company quickly ex-
panded. At *WrestleMania VII* in 1991, he defeated Jimmy
Snuka with a trademark Tombstone Piledriver. The match

lasted barely four minutes, but it initiated a storied and un-matched string of victories at wrestling's annual event.

Undertaker was injured in 1993 and had to take time off from professional wrestling. At *WrestleMania* in 1994, an-other Undertaker was introduced to the crowd but quickly denounced as "Underfaker." The real Undertaker returned, reclaiming sole (no pun intended) possession of the charac-ter in a face-off at that year's *SummerSlam*. From that point on, his character grew in popularity.

KANE

In October 1997, a new phenom exploded onto the scene—Kane, Undertaker's younger brother. At seven feet, three hundred and twenty-five pounds, Kane was a big hit—in more ways than one.

BROTHERLY UNLOVE

One other person played a key role in the showdown: Paul Bearer. He had been Undertaker's manager and sidekick practically from the moment he made his debut. Now he became Undertaker's nemesis—and was arguably more dan-gerous than any of the men Undertaker had met in the ring.

Paul Bearer laid the groundwork for the clash over a series of weeks at the end of 1997, appearing on a number of *Raw* episodes and announcing with great portentousness that he was about to rock Undertaker's undead world.

At the time, Undertaker was busy pursuing Shawn Mi-chaels for a championship title. Michaels, aided by D-Gen-eration X, was at the top of the company's wrestling hierarchy, holding the championship title and enjoying enormous pop-ularity with the crowd.

Michaels and Undertaker met in a Hell in a Cell match at *Badd Blood* in October 1997, just in time for Halloween.

Hell in the Cell matches are a more refined—and according to many, more dangerous—version of Steel Cage matches. The addition of a top confines the wrestlers to the ring, and, in theory at least, there's no way to win the match by disqualification. Undertaker devised the cell after his attempts to seek satisfaction with Michaels were foiled by run-ins by Michaels's allies.

Even though both wrestlers tangled outside of the cage, Undertaker's strategy worked, and he topped Michaels at the end of a brutal match, flattening him with a steel chair.

Just as he was about to press the unconscious Michaels's shoulders to the mat for the pin, the lights in the arena went out. Paul Bearer emerged from the backstage area . . . escorting a masked friend: Kane.

Kane ripped the door from the cage and confronted a stunned Undertaker. For probably the first time in his career, Undertaker found himself looking up to another wrestler (though they're both billed at seven feet, Kane appeared taller in this match).

Mimicking Undertaker's own trademark move, Kane threw his arms down, conjuring flames from torches at the corners of the ring. He then applied a Tombstone Piledriver to the still unbelieving Undertaker.

Shawn Michaels was able to crawl forward and throw his nearly lifeless arm over his opponent for the win. But the fans' real interest was clearly going to be the brother-versus-brother story line.

RAISING KANE

The Piledriver initiated bitter feelings over the next few months — and in many ways over the next several years, since the story line has been revived numerous times in different ways.

Kane didn't speak in the early going, leaving Paul Bearer to lay out the story. According to the manager-turned-enemy, Undertaker's parents had died in a tragic fire. Kane — Undertaker's *half* brother, according to Paul Bearer — had been horribly burned in the same fire but managed to survive. The mask he wore hid his scars; his preoccupation with fire was a natural outgrowth of his childhood experience.

Undertaker had never hidden the fact that the fire had killed his parents, but he had never acknowledged setting it. According to Paul Bearer, Undertaker had blamed his baby brother, Kane.

The secret was so hideous that many fans refused to believe it. Paul Bearer would eventually claim to have nursed Kane back to health, though as the story developed he kept his reasons for doing so to himself.

Despite provocations, Undertaker steadily refused to wrestle Kane. He was unwilling to risk harming his brother again.

ROYAL RUMBLE 1998 CASKET MATCH

From the moment of his debut, Kane rocketed to popularity, even before he actually wrestled anyone. He spent several weeks attacking different wrestlers, until finally he fought at the November Pay-Per-View, *Survivor Series*, beating Mankind.

Still, the fight everyone wanted to see was between the brothers. That looked as if it would never come off as the two men reconciled, or appeared to. Kane began backing his brother at matches, possibly, the crowd thought, because of Undertaker's principled stance against harming him.

Shawn Michaels and Undertaker prepared for a rematch at the *Royal Rumble 1998*. Once again, a unique format was invented just for their confrontation—a Casket match. In order to win, a wrestler had to throw his opponent into the casket and close the lid on him.

Despite some underhanded tricks by Michaels, Undertaker dominated into the middle of the match, until a Piledriver by Michaels outside the ring left Undertaker vulnerable to a run-in by DX. Michaels was able to roll Undertaker into the casket, seemingly clinching the victory.

For the undead, caskets are veritable fountains of youth. As soon as he touched the coffin's cushioned lining, Undertaker revived. Back in the ring, Michaels once more got the upper hand. But the match depended on him depositing Undertaker in the casket—and once more, Undertaker regained energy there.

The match seemed nearly over as Undertaker took control and dumped Michaels into the coffin. Before he could slam the lid, a half dozen wrestlers appeared and began stomping him. The lights went out with Undertaker on the canvas.

Kane appeared, rising from the back—or perhaps the jaws of hell—with a burst of flame. He exorcised DX from the ring. Within seconds, only the two brothers were left in the ring.

This was no time for a brotherly hug. With Michaels slinking away in the background, Kane began smacking

Undertaker around, to the boos of the crowd. A chokeslam sent Undertaker into the casket and gave Michaels the victory.

But the worst was still to come.

DEAD AGAIN

Kane and Paul Bearer locked the casket, then wheeled it away from the ring and down the runway. Kane retrieved an ax.

It took nearly a dozen smacks with the ax to punch through the top. Paul Bearer came out with a jug of gasoline. In seconds, the coffin was ablaze.

He who was undead was dead again.

HE'S BACK . . .

Undertaker vanished, and it appeared as if he really was dead and buried, if not forgotten. Michaels, meanwhile, dropped his title to Steve Austin and took time off to heal from his injuries . . . though not before he spoofed Undertaker's return on *Raw*, dressing as the Dead Man and then throwing off his disguise in the ring to the hoots and howls of the crowd.

A week or two later, the real Undertaker returned. Summoned by the peal of Undertaker's trademark bells, a lightning bolt struck his coffin, and the Dead Man was freed to once more walk the earth. The only walking he wanted to do now was over his brother's grave. But of course the fight couldn't take place without a bit more buildup.

Paul Bearer and Kane continued to torment Undertaker, digging up his father's and mother's coffins, desecrating their graves as well as their memory. In March, the brothers faced off at *WrestleMania XIV* with a pyrotechnics show that still ranks as one of the most impressive indoor displays ever.

WRESTLEMANIA XIV

Led by his Druids from the underworld, Undertaker strode slowly to the ring, his samurai-like cape designating him the high priest of immortal fiends. Kane, looking a bit nervous, met his brother in the ring. As the match started, they exchanged a series of punches and fist slaps. Encouraged when Undertaker's onslaught failed to move him, Kane mounted a vicious attack, managing to hoist Undertaker upside down on the turnbuckle and inflicting as much punishment as any of his previous opponents.

The fight moved out of the ring, where Paul Bearer was able to get in his own cheap shots, helping Kane dominate. A sizable portion of the audience was behind Kane, and it seemed as if Undertaker would actually lose his first *WrestleMania*.

An exhausted Undertaker tried mounting a comeback and managed to drop Kane from the ring. Gathering his strength, he leaped out at him—and missed, cratering one of the commentators' tables instead.

Kane flew to the advantage as the fight resumed between the ropes. He appeared to beat Undertaker with a pin, at least by Paul Bearer's quick count. As the ref waved off the accomplice's count, saying Undertaker had kicked out at two, the combatants began a series of moves that saw Undertaker give his brother three different piledrivers before the last took Kane's breath away.

It led to a pin, and a victory for Undertaker.

Paul Bearer wasn't content to let things rest there. He entered the ring, trying to pummel the weakened Dead Man whom he had once managed. Undertaker still had enough fight to flatten him.

But it was Kane who had the last laugh and arguably the most devastating hit in the contest.

With his brother preoccupied, he grabbed the chair Paul Bearer had brought into the ring and laid Undertaker out on the canvas. Then he hobbled away in silence. The crowd had turned back in Undertaker's favor, turned off by Kane's treachery.

SURROUNDED BY FIRE

Topping the epic contest would not be easy, but with fans eager for more, a rematch was inevitable.

The following week, the pair fought at *Mayhem in Manchester*, a United Kingdom Pay-Per-View. (Undertaker was wearing street clothes, unusual for him at the time.) Undertaker won the match in a pin.

The match was broadcast only in the United Kingdom, and audiences in the United States and elsewhere had to wait until *In Your House: Unforgiven*, held in St. Louis at the end of April 1998.

Once more, Undertaker was involved in a unique-style match: The ring was surrounded by a wall of fire. To win, a wrestler had to set his opponent on fire. Since that was the only criterion for victory and anything you could do to your opponent was legal, there was no ref inside with the wrestlers.

For much of the match, the twenty thousand people attending were silent, clearly awed by the flames and the inherent danger. Even Kane seemed to be taken aback when, after Undertaker climbed onto the top rope near the beginning of the match, the flames shot up several feet.

The action was slow early on but began heating up,

literally and figuratively, after Undertaker tossed Kane over the flames and out of the ring.

Apparently having had enough, Kane began to retreat toward the locker room. Paul Bearer ran to the flame control and jacked it so high that Undertaker couldn't get out of the ring to follow. Then Kane's escape was cut off by Vader (who would later ally with Undertaker as a tag team partner). Undertaker gathered himself and leaped over the flames, then ran and knocked out his brother. With Kane down, he chased Paul Bearer into the audience—it was a slow-motion chase—finally cornering him on the band's stage. He crowned his tormenter with a drum, then returned to settle the score with his brother.

Both wrestlers were still outside the ring. Undertaker was able to win by holding Kane's hand in the fire. Kane ran from the arena, vanquished.

PAUL BEARER IS THE FATHER

The story line took a new turn the next night at *Raw*, when an inadvertent airing of a backstage conversation revealed that Paul Bearer was Kane's father.

That was bad enough, but once the secret was out, Paul Bearer told Undertaker that his mother was nothing but a "two-bit whore."

Undertaker vented his feelings rather physically on both Bearer and Kane over the next few weeks.

After Kane beat Undertaker on *Raw*—June 1, 1998—the feud between the brothers mutated into new forms, as longtime Undertaker nemesis Stone Cold Steve Austin worked into a story with (and against) Undertaker. When the pair were forced to work together as tag team allies,

Undertaker's loyalties were questioned as blood triumphed over water.

Or more accurately, given Austin was involved, beer.

On July, at *In Your House 23*, Stone Cold teamed with Undertaker to take on Kane and Mankind. The uneasy alliance—at one point, Undertaker gave Austin the finger rather than going for the pin on his brother—brought them the tag team title, though of course the alliance was suitably short-lived.

REBIRTH . . . TIMES SEVERAL

The Kane-Undertaker story has seen several reincarnations, with the brothers working together and then falling apart. One of the most notable installments revolved around *WrestleMania XX*.

Undertaker and Mr. McMahon squared off in a Buried Alive match at *Survivor Series* in the fall of 2003. Thanks to a run-in by Kane, McMahon won and buried Undertaker. For some time, it seemed as if Undertaker was gone for good, as he disappeared from the weekly show.

But then dreams of his brother began haunting Kane. He lost focus and control in his matches as the episodes continued. His brother was calling for revenge from beyond the grave.

Kane was never one to scare easily. At *WrestleMania XX* in March 2004, he reverted to character, screaming at the audience that he had killed his brother because "he became one of *you*."

Then a bong began to ring through Madison Square Garden. Unexpectedly, Paul Bearer had returned to Undertaker's corner, and he led him and his torch-carrying escort back to the ring for the match. Few wrestlers, alive or dead, were as over with the crowd as Undertaker was that night. The chants for Undertaker probably woke up half of the corpses in New Jersey's cemeteries across the river, as the fans showed who their favorite was.

Undertaker won with a Tombstone Piledriver, still his signature finish, then gave the crowd the evil eye, as undead as ever.

STEVE AUSTIN
VS. MR. McMAHON

S how me someone who's never wanted to punch the boss in the mouth, and I'll show you someone who's never held a job.

There was a bit more to the rivalry but that was really the emotion that drove the conflict between Steve Austin and Mr. McMahon over a roughly four-year period starting in late 1997. It didn't hurt that Austin was at the top of his game, or that McMahon had already achieved a great deal of notoriety both inside and outside the wrestling business. As soon as one entered the arena, fans began looking for the other—anticipating a brutal showdown.

"A RAT'S ASS"

In his book *Stone Cold Truth*, Austin dates the conflict from the January 1998 lead-in to *WrestleMania*, but in reality things got going in the fall of 1997, during a time when Austin wasn't actually wrestling.

The star's neck had been broken in a match with Owen Hart at *SummerSlam* at the beginning of August 1997. The injury was highly publicized and discussed not just on *Raw* but in the mainstream media. It wasn't clear for quite a while whether the damage could be repaired, or what Austin's future would be.

But as far as Stone Cold was concerned, there was no room for discussion or debate. He wanted to wrestle more than anything. He was a badass who didn't take crap from nobody, not even the doctors.

Not even his boss, if his boss was backing the doctors.

Austin and Mr. McMahon confronted each other on *Raw* at the end of September 1997. Despite his injury, Austin demanded that he be allowed to get back in the ring.

Mr. McMahon thought the injury was too severe. Austin was a nut and out of control.

"It stops right now," declared Mr. McMahon. No way he was letting Austin wrestle.

"You're trying to lay down the law on Steve Austin?" answered the wrestler. "It sounds like you're trying to fire me. Go ahead, big shot. Because I don't give a rat's ass what you do."

Mr. McMahon gave Austin the option of signing a release absolving the company of any liability if he got hurt wrestling.

"If I wanted to, I'd snap that collection of diamonds you call a neck," said Austin. "Bring your little paper out here. Maybe I'll sign it, and maybe I'll shove it up your little ass."

Austin also promised to beat up Mr. McMahon if he fired him.

He walked off after giving Mr. McMahon a Steve Austin salute: a pair of middle fingers in the face.

SIGN LANGUAGE FOR MIKE TYSON

Austin got surgery and was cleared to wrestle. Before coming back full-time, he made a string of appearances delivering stunners to wrestlers he didn't like—a large group, given his general disposition.

But it was his conflict with Mr. McMahon that would suddenly flare. The next spark came with the announcement on *Raw* in mid-January 1998 that world heavyweight boxing champion Mike Tyson would be part of that year's *Wrestle-Mania*, scheduled for the end of March.

Mr. McMahon told the *Raw* audience that Tyson would be a "special enforcer," hired to make sure the main event was fair.

The announcement was interrupted by Stone Cold Steve Austin, who demanded "a piece of Mike Tyson's ass."

Austin didn't like the fact that the boxer had invaded the wrestling world and had the audacity to call himself "the baddest man on the planet" in his house. Austin considered himself the baddest man on the planet, and he wasn't going to abide any interlopers.

"Don't say one word, Vince," Austin told Mr. McMahon. "I'll knock you down, too."

Austin then told Tyson, who was hardly a universally loved figure, that he could beat him any day of the week, and twice on Sunday.

He repeated the message in sign language, with a finger from each hand.

Tyson shoved him across the ring. All hell broke loose. Austin was dragged away.

The show was on.

"YELLOW BASTARD"

Austin had won the right to vie for the championship title at the *Royal Rumble* in January 1998, surviving a thirty-man rumble to secure the slot against Shawn Michaels, who'd reigned as champion since the Montreal Screwjob a few months before.

DX and Michaels suggested that Austin take on Tyson at *WrestleMania*—in fact they campaigned for it on one *Raw* show—but the championship belt was on Michaels, and that remained Austin's focus.

Michaels's allies in DX harassed Austin during the weeks that followed, ambushing him and tying him up. Austin retaliated, and blood boiled as the feud built toward *Wrestle-Mania*. At the February Pay-Per-View, *No Way Out*, Austin and pals—Cactus Jack, Owen Hart, and Chainsaw Charlie—defeated a DX team led by Triple H.

The conflict amped on *Raw* in March. On the March 2 show, Michaels tore Tyson's shirt off, revealing a DX T-shirt. Tyson was supposed to be neutral, but his defection to the heel stable made Michaels the odds-on favorite to retain the championship.

Austin blamed Mr. McMahon for Tyson's treachery, calling him a "yellow bastard." Many fans thought that Mr. McMahon was setting Austin up for a fall, and that Tyson, so obviously in DX's corner, would hand the match to Michaels. Given that the Montreal Screwjob had taken place only a few months before, it seemed almost logical.

Michaels managed to get sucker kicks in on Austin during two different shows, laying Stone Cold down as the tension ramped up. Meanwhile, Michaels was nursing a serious back injury that ultimately had required surgery and in fact wasn't fully healed when the bell rang at *WrestleMania*.

A "REAL" HEEL

Mr. McMahon had no shades of gray, no coolness that might soften his image. He was not just a boss—he was a tyrannical boss, an out-and-out asshole, likely to pull any deal he wanted and wrap the title belt around whoever kowtowed the most.

Anyone with any grievance against his or her employer had no trouble identifying with those who opposed Mr. McMahon.

Especially when they did it with the verve and style of the "bionic redneck," Stone Cold Steve Austin.

WRESTLEMANIA

The 1998 *WrestleMania* was held in Boston. Tickets to the event sold out in two minutes, a record at the time.

The conflict built right up to the event. Austin was tied up by DX at a workout on the City Hall Plaza in Boston. Tyson made no secret of his allegiance, helping to taunt the Rattlesnake.

When the lights went down for *WrestleMania*, Tyson appeared with a DX "Suck it" T-shirt and was booed soundly by the crowd. Stone Cold, wearing his simple jean trunks and vest, brought the Boston Garden crowd to its feet in a massive roar.

The reception for Michaels's entrance, accompanied by a rap-rock band, was subdued by contrast. The crowd's chant for Stone Cold nearly drowned out the music. The combatants began by walking around each other, exchanging a few punches. Despite his injury, Michaels was soon bouncing around the ring, flying out and landing on Triple H on the ring apron.

Michaels's DX stablemates put Austin into one of the barriers when he came out of the ring. Triple H and Chyna were ordered away from the ring by Tyson, giving the crowd the first hint that he might be more neutral than they supposed.

Despite DX, Austin dominated Michaels through most of the early going, even though Michaels managed to kick out from attempted pins again and again. Tyson, with several opportunities to interfere on Michaels's behalf outside the ring, stayed back.

After fifteen minutes or so, Michaels rallied, punching Austin against the ropes and on the canvas. But it takes more than fists and feet to kill a Texas rattlesnake.

Using the rope for leverage, Michaels pressed a figure-four leglock on Austin but couldn't win a submission or a pin. Austin turned the hold, reversing the pressure so that it was Michaels who was in trouble.

A break, a catapult into the ropes, a sleeper—the match seesawed back and forth until the referee was caught against the turnbuckle and knocked out. Austin grabbed Michaels and began stomping him in the corner. Tyson, who could have used the ref's knockdown as an excuse to come in as the replacement, remained outside. With a furious show, Michaels rallied and sent Austin to the canvas.

The champ began warming up for his Sweet Chin Music finish, but Austin rose from the dead. Spinning, he applied his own signature move, the Stone Cold Stunner.

Michaels fell to the canvas. Stone Cold covered—and Mike Tyson jumped into the ring and counted Michaels down. Austin was the new champion.

THE HARD WAY

The *WrestleMania* showdown was part of a larger set of confrontations between Austin and Mr. McMahon that continued that year. Mr. McMahon did not want Steve Austin as the champion of the company because he was too low class, too trashy, to serve as the company's standard-bearer.

Mr. McMahon was also afraid of him, though that was generally not stated explicitly. Instead, Mr. McMahon told Austin not to get violent, cringing with every word.

On the *Raw* show immediately after *WrestleMania*, Mr. McMahon presented Austin with the title belt. After some back-and-forth during which Mr. McMahon took back statements that he didn't want Austin as champ, Austin made Mr. McMahon demonstrate his "love" by proclaiming how much he liked him.

McMahon had trouble raising his voice above a whisper. It grew louder, however, when he used it to give Austin a lecture on how he had to be flexible and not always do things the hard way.

Austin asked the audience what they thought.

Hard way?

Hell, yeah!

He gave Mr. McMahon a Stunner and walked off with a smile.

A NEW MAN: THE OLD MAN

Later in the show, Mr. McMahon had Austin arrested—not an easy task for the officers involved, though they accomplished it. The following week on *Raw*, Mr. McMahon announced that Austin was now a new man: no more beer drinking in the ring, no more blue jean shorts, nothing but a clean-cut, good-guy image.

Sure enough, out came Austin, wearing a suit.

Naturally, this didn't last too long, all of maybe two minutes.

"Take a picture of the suit," Austin told Mr. McMahon, "because it's the last time you'll see it."

He ripped off the suit and said he'd change for no one.

Austin asked the crowd at the April 14 *Raw* if they wanted an Austin-McMahon match.

Hell, yeah!

A short time later, Mr. McMahon appeared in wrestling gear. Austin had claimed he could take Mr. McMahon with one hand tied behind his back, and Mr. McMahon demanded he make good.

Just as the match was about to come off, Dude Love appeared. He claimed he was a peacemaker but eventually got into a fight with both men, setting the stage for a match between himself and Austin at *Unforgiven* later that month.

UNFORGIVEN

After a match mostly dominated by Austin, the two wrestlers knocked out the referee. Dude Love then got the better of Austin, putting him down and out on the canvas.

Mr. McMahon, who'd been sitting at ringside, came over and tried to revive the referee so he could count the fall. But the ref remained out of it, and Dude Love missed his chance. Austin rallied, then followed Dude out of the ring. The wrestlers exchanged chair shots, one of which put Mr. McMahon out. Austin threw Dude back into the ring, pinned him, and counted him out himself.

Austin left the arena. An official, Gerald Brisco, came into the ring, declared that Austin had been disqualified for hitting a promotion official (Mr. McMahon), and gave the decision to Dude Love.

A rematch was set for May 2, 1998, at *In Your House: Over*

the Edge, the Pay-Per-View held in Milwaukee that year. The odds were immediately stacked against Austin, as Mr. McMahon named himself the special referee.

This time, Dude Love took out Mr. McMahon (accidentally) with a chair. When Austin laid him out a short time later, he lifted McMahon's hand himself to count out his opponent.

WHAT DID HE *REALLY* THINK?

The Austin–Mr. McMahon conflict continued over the next three and half years or so, simmering for a while before erupting again. Austin tormented Mr. McMahon in a deliciously uneven fight, always managing to get the last word.

Every viewer probably has his or her own favorite episode: the time Austin attacked Mr. McMahon in the hospital, the time he filled his sports car with cement, the time he gave him a beer washing in the Philadelphia ring. A highlight reel could fill several hours.

Now that he no longer wrestles, Austin calls Vince McMahon a friend. He also paid him the ultimate wrestling compliment, saying he was a tough S.O.B. and a true professional.

But what did he think of him as a *boss*?

In several shows, Austin kicked Mr. McMahon in the midsection as part of the act. At least a few hit somewhat lower than the belt.

"Sometimes my shorts or jeans were too tight, depending on my weight situation," he claims, "and I couldn't lift my leg high enough. Any time I kicked him below the belt, it was not intentional."

He must have had an awful lot of "weight situations," judging from the videos.

9

TRIPLE H
VS. THE ROCK

In the beginning, Triple H and The Rock were two self-obsessed heels, strivers at the bottom of the mountain looking to climb up. Before too long, each would arrive at the pinnacle of professional wrestling success, wearing the championship belt. But to get there, they had to go over—and through—each other.

HUNTER HEARST-HELMSLEY

Hunter Hearst-Helmsley, a rich, wellborn Connecticut snot, joined World Wrestling Federation in 1995. At first, fans hated him because of his money and stuck-up ways. But soon they had other reasons: his snarl, his underhanded tricks, his viciousness. Even so, Triple H was a great wrestler, and his "cool" demeanor won him a growing following. By the fall of 1996, Triple H—the nickname by which his character quickly became known—was vying for the Intercontinental Championship. He took the title in October, holding it for four months before being challenged by Rocky Maivia, aka The Rock.

ROCKY "THE ROCK" MAIVIA

The son of professional wrestler Rocky "Soul Man" Johnson, The Rock—also known as Rocky Maivia in the ring—began wrestling after a professional football career failed to gain much traction. Giving up a spot on a Canadian team's practice squad, Johnson turned to wrestling in 1996.

His career choice should have come as no surprise. Besides his father, Johnson is related to a string of Samoan wrestlers, including Afa and Sika Anoa'I, and is the grandson of High Chief Pete Maivia, making him a third-generation wrestler.

His outstanding wrestling pedigree and clean-cut look helped lift him ahead of more established wrestlers, and he was soon aiming for the Intercontinental title. The showdown between The Rock and Triple H was an inevitable clash of styles and demeanors.

IN YOUR HOUSE 1997

The pair met in back-to-back events in February 1997, first on a special Thursday edition of *Raw*, and then at the *In Your House* Pay-Per-View a few nights later.

Both matches were high-octane, energetic affairs, won by Rock. The wrestlers put on an athletic display, and the crowds at both events saw a number of wild flights across the ring.

Though in theory the bad guy, Triple H got plenty of applause from the crowd at *In Your House* as he dominated the early part of the bout. But Rock kept getting up, rising almost from the dead to face off against his opponent.

Eight minutes into the second match, the crowd began to chant for The Rock. With his heat building, Rock tried to finish off Triple H. Each time he failed, until finally Goldust appeared, distracting Triple H long enough for Rock to set up a suplex and then get the pin to retain the title he'd won a few nights before.

THE ROCK GETS 'TUDE

This was The Attitude Era, and Rock's clean-cut image, and possibly the fact that he was a newcomer to the sport who'd rocketed to the top, didn't go over very well with a portion of the fans. He began hearing boos and assorted "Rocky sucks" chants.

Injuries forced a brief layoff. When he returned, Rock came back with a much more aggressive edge. He joined the Nation of Domination, a faction led by Faarooq. Then he started calling himself "The Rock" and speaking in the third person.

"The Rock says . . ." became his favorite tagline, as week after week he proclaimed his greatness. Eventually, other words and phrases entered his lexicon, and that of wrestling in general. Among them: *jabroni* (ignorant jerk who doesn't appreciate The Rock's greatness), *monkey crap* (pretty much what it says), *Smackdown hotel* (the beating The Rock will administer), and *Do you smell what The Rock is cooking?*

The more fans chanted "Rocky sucks," the more he liked it. Eventually, their ire turned to grudging admiration, and The Rock became one of the most popular wrestlers in the company.

DX'D

Triple H, meanwhile, had found his inner heel as the co-leader of D-Generation X. It was only natural that DX and the Nation would eventually tangle. When they mixed it up, their leading figures came to blows.

The Rock had regained the Intercontinental title. Triple H wanted it for himself. They went against each other for the title at the July 1998 Pay-Per-View, *In Your House: Fully Loaded*.

The match was a Two-Out-of-Three Falls decision, meaning that one of the wrestlers needed to make two pins to win. It ended in a draw, allowing The Rock to hold his title.

The next night on *Raw*, Triple H was joined by DX stablemate X-Pac (Sean Waltman) in a three-way contest against The Rock for another shot at the championship. This match ended in frustration as The Rock left the arena while the two DX members argued, thus retaining the title on a disqualification.

Despite the conflict, DX remained intact, largely due to its continuing conflict with the Nation. A street fight at the August 17 *Raw* featured some one-on-one action between the two leaders; the following week, The Rock took the lead in humiliating Triple H's manager and girlfriend, Chyna, backstage.

After forcing Chyna to her knees, The Rock told Chyna that he wouldn't kiss a piece of "trash" like her—his sidekick Mark Henry would do it. Shawn Michaels came to the rescue, freeing Chyna and cementing DX's popularity with the fans.

SUMMERSLAM 1998

Though champion, The Rock continued to hear loud "Rocky sucks" chants during the early stages of his match against Triple H the following week at *SummerSlam*.

The Ladder match was a relatively slow contest, at least by the two wrestlers' usual standards. Triple H was dragging an injured knee through much of the fight. The Rock began pounding on the knee early in the match, lodging it into the ladder and slamming it with a chair.

Though badly bruised, Triple H managed to rebound and knock The Rock from the ladder just as he reached for the championship belt. He was too depleted to turn this into a lasting advantage, and The Rock abused him for several minutes, finally giving him a back drop onto the ladder outside the ring.

Another rally returned Triple H to the ring, where he managed to get off a baseball slide and knock the ladder into The Rock's face. Bloodied, The Rock began to stagger.

Both men exchanged punches and topples from the rungs. Chyna snuck a chair to Triple H and decked Mark Henry outside the ring. But she couldn't keep Henry, billed as the "World's Strongest Man," from helping his Nation ally.

When Henry threw powder into Triple H's eyes, the wrestler was forced to climb the ladder blind. The Rock raced up the other side. As his fingers touched the title belt, Chyna climbed between the ropes and took revenge for the previous week's humiliations by slugging The Rock in the gonads. As he toppled to the canvas, Triple H grasped the title belt and pulled it down for the championship.

A BREAK

While Triple H took time off to heal his leg, The Rock continued his climb, taking the World Wrestling Federation Championship at *Survivor Series* in November. The two briefly faced off over the title in January 1999, when The Rock won an I Quit match on *Raw* to retain the title.

An I Quit match ends when one of the wrestlers says those words; in this case, Triple H was moved to resign because of a threat by Kane to chokeslam Chyna.

By now, The Rock was part of Mr. McMahon's personal stable, the Corporation, which was warring with DX. The dominating factor in World Wrestling Federation, at this time, was the McMahon family's dysfunction, with the various members of the wrestling company's ownership arguing with and occasionally beating the pants off each other. Mr. McMahon and his son Shane were the first to tangle, but eventually Mr. McMahon's daughter Stephanie and his wife, Linda, got involved as well. There were various permutations and alliances through 1999 and into 2000 and 2001.

The dysfunction among family members came to a head at *WrestleMania XVI*, where each McMahon was represented by a different wrestler in a Four-Way Elimination match. The Rock had Vince McMahon in his corner, Triple H had Stephanie, and Big Show (Shane) and Mick Foley (Linda) rounded out the competition.

Triple H was the champion, and his title was on the line at the headliner. All four wrestlers had been tangling in the months leading up to the meet; at a pair of matches at *No Way Out* in February, Big Show had earned his shot at the title by downing The Rock, and Triple H forced Foley to retire by beating him in his match. (Foley was brought back for *WrestleMania* by Linda McMahon, who declared it was only fair.)

The *WrestleMania* match came down to The Rock and Triple H. With both wrestlers staggering, Shane McMahon climbed into the ring. It wasn't clear whom he was going to help—his champion, Big Show, had already been eliminated. It remained unclear even as his father ran over and decked him.

The Rock got up and seemed primed for a win, especially since his backer was in the ring. But Mr. McMahon proceeded to take down The Rock as well, giving the victory to Triple H.

BACKLASH

Angry that he had been denied the title, The Rock got up and bounced Mr. McMahon, then gave Stephanie a Rock Bottom and the People's Elbow (two of his signature moves) after she attempted to intervene.

The crowd loved it. The turn had made The Rock back into a good guy—and a popular one.

The match set up a reconciliation of sorts among the McMahon factions; more important, it prepared the way for another Rock–Triple H showdown at *Backlash* the following month.

This time, Shane McMahon was working as ref, something that obviously helped Triple H. When he finally couldn't take the one-sided interference any longer, The Rock put him and Triple H through one of the announcers' tables. Distracted by Mr. McMahon, The Rock was surprised by Triple H, who incapacitated him with a Pedigree, normally his finisher.

"Rock-y! Rock-y!" yelled the fans as The Rock struggled to his feet.

With Shane down, Mr. McMahon called for a substitute ref. Two raced to the ring, where they promptly pounced on The Rock. It looked like another bad ending for the man who called himself the People's Champ and the Brahma Bull, but just then Stone Cold Steve Austin made a surprise appearance, racing from backstage and clearing the ring. Linda McMahon appeared, called in another ref, and The Rock got the pin.

And the traditional Steve Austin beer chug in celebration of the win.

BACK TO TRIPLE H

The feud between The Rock and Triple H had been going on for several months, but it had only reached its midpoint. At *Judgment Day 2000* in May, the two wrestlers competed in an epic sixty-minute Iron Man match. (In an Iron Man match, the winner is the wrestler with the most falls to his credit during the time limit.) Shawn Michaels, clearly leaning toward Triple H, was the guest referee.

The match seesawed back and forth, picking up steam as the time went on. Triple H took a commanding 5–3 lead with less than fifteen minutes to go. The Rock fought back until, with both wrestlers nearing exhaustion and roughly ninety seconds left, he managed to tie the score at 5.

Triple H had been worn down and looked too weak to continue. Mr. McMahon appeared, and with the aid of X-Pac and other Corporation members, reversed the momentum by beating the lights out of The Rock. But before any of the attackers could drape Triple H over The Rock for a pin (and the win), Undertaker appeared, clearing the ring of McMahon and his cronies.

It wasn't enough to give The Rock a victory. Michaels ruled that the interference disqualified Rock, which gave Triple H the win, 6–5.

FINALE

The final match in this round of The Rock–Triple H saga came the following month at *King of the Ring 2000*, where the two antagonists were joined by allies—Undertaker and Kane in The Rock's case, and Mr. McMahon and his son Shane in Triple H's—in a six-man event.

Early on, the two McMahons took turns getting pounded, as all three of their opponents unloaded on them. Then the uneasy alliance between The Rock and his partners began to break down.

Just as The Rock readied a pin on Triple H, Kane interrupted by chokeslamming him to the mat. When Triple H seemed to welcome the new alliance, Kane attacked him. The Rock and his undead allies once more united. A Rock Bottom to Mr. McMahon ended the match. The Rock took the championship belt in hand, ending the long-running feud.

TALKING THE TALK

Run-ins and complications characterized the showdown between The Rock and Triple H during their epic struggle. This was typical of the era, where the only thing viewers could be sure of was that there was nothing they could be sure of.

What was truly special, though, was the wrestlers' way with words, The Rock especially. Talking about himself in the third person, The Rock would get his mouth going at a rapid pace, spewing perfect sentences and even paragraphs as he verbally lacerated his opponents.

Triple H answered tit for tat, but his most potent response came not from his mouth but from his eyes—his stare downs were the visual equivalent of The Rock's verbiage, as unnerving as any put-down.

MATCH OR NO MATCH

Even when The Rock and Triple H weren't directly confronting each other in a match, the two added considerable heat to the proceedings. At *SummerSlam 2002*, Brock Lesnar aimed to take The Rock's championship title. On *Raw* in Seattle, two weeks before the match, Triple H talked up Lesnar before the crowd.

Suddenly The Rock appeared. The crowd went wild. Confronting Lesnar, The Rock promised an ass whooping.

"Who the hell do you think you are?" asked Triple H.

"I am the Brahma Bull, the People's Champ, the Undisputed Champion, something you're not. . . . So shut up, bitch."

"You left out one thing. You're the guy who's going to get his ass whooped if you walk into this ring."

Clearly on The Rock's side, the crowd tried to shout down Triple H with a chant of "ass-hole."

"Let me get this straight," said The Rock, climbing into the ring. "You want to go?"

"I would love to go."

More than the words, their faces showed pure hate. The

fans picked up on the electricity. They went at it, street clothes and all. Triple H got the better of The Rock that night, laying him out with a Pedigree.

OUT OF THE HOUSE

Soon after their showdown ended, The Rock shifted his career focus to acting, though he continued to wrestle with WWE. Their trash-talk-laced series of showdowns remains one of the more entertaining, if complicated, confrontations in recent wrestling history.

10

THE ROCK VS. STEVE AUSTIN

One of the reasons Stone Cold Steve Austin became a Superstar in the late 1990s was the quality of the opponents he faced. Among the best was The Rock, who matched up against him at three *WrestleManias*, and in countless other shows along the way.

The matchups were natural. Both men were at the top of their game. Both were proud of who they were and hated anything that stepped in their path. Their different races made the matches even more volatile.

CHAMPION-INTERRUPTUS

After winning the Intercontinental Championship from Owen Hart in 1997, Stone Cold had to take a break from wrestling because of a neck injury. When he came back, The Rock waltzed into the ring and interrupted his speech to the fans.

"I hate to rain on your little victory parade," The Rock

told Stone Cold as the audience booed. "Everybody knows that when I was World Wrestling Federation Intercontinental Champion, I was the best damn Intercontinental Champion there ever was!"

More boos. Even louder.

"Stone Cold Steve Austin, I'm challenging you for the Intercontinental Championship, and if you have any manhood at all, you'll accept my challenge."

Even more boos.

"If you accept my challenge, then your bottom line will say: 'Stone Cold—has been. Compliments of . . . The Rock.' "

The boos shook the building so severely, it seemed the roof would cave in.

"SO SPECIAL"

In his memoir on wrestling, The Rock summed up why the matches were so great:

> *The Rock detests Stone Cold Steve Austin. The Rock realizes that Stone Cold Steve Austin is without a doubt the biggest piece of Texas trailer-park trash walking God's green earth. Why does The Rock feel this way? Because the guy personifies what trash would be to The Rock. He's the exact opposite of The Rock. . . . And you know what? Stone Cold hates The Rock right back, which is fine with The Rock, because that's what makes their rivalry so special.*

The two wrestlers exchanged a whole lot of trash talking in the following weeks. The Rock, still known to many fans as Rocky, claimed that he was the real champion and even showed off a championship belt in the ring on *Raw*.

Stone Cold upped the ante, paging The Rock while he was strutting in the middle of the ring. The Rock looked down at his beeper, trying to figure out what sort of emergency led someone to call him in the middle of a prime-time TV broadcast.

The number on the beeper was 3-1-6.

Or 3:16.

Before The Rock could register his anger, he was downed by a Stone Cold Stunner.

IN YOUR HOUSE

The pair met at the December 1997 Pay-Per-View, *In Your House 19: D-Generation X.*

The Rock entered to a chant of "Rocky sucks!"

"Finally, the time has come for The Rock to defend his Intercontinental title," he answered, whistling past the boos.

Stone Cold drove into the arena in his pickup truck. The Rock's friends in the Nation gave Austin a harsh reception, softening him up before the match began. But Stone Cold persevered and, as soon as the match began, started wailing on his proper opponent.

"Austin came to fight; he didn't come to wrestle," said legendary WWE announcer Jim "J.R." Ross.

Austin was on fire. Even when the Nation wrestlers jumped him, Stone Cold dented heads—and his pickup— and put them down.

With things going against him, The Rock resorted to a time-honored tactic—a pair of brass knuckles "magically" appeared in his hand. When he tried to use them to inscribe his name on Stone Cold's skull, Austin took him down with a Stunner.

The end was quick. With the ref knocked out during the action a new ref jumped in and counted The Rock down. The audience exploded.

The match helped solidify Austin's position as wrestling's most important Superstar. It also cemented The Rock's status. He was now on the top rung of worthy challengers in the company, a guy fans could get excited about hating.

They would have plenty of opportunity.

THE PEOPLE'S CHAMPION

Things were just starting to heat up between The Rock and Stone Cold. The next night on *Raw*, as part of the Mr. McMahon–Stone Cold story line, Mr. McMahon claimed that the ref had been about to disqualify Stone Cold and ordered Stone Cold to give The Rock a rematch. (Referees took it especially hard during Stone Cold–The Rock matchups. Few remained on their feet for the whole match.)

Shock of shocks, Austin—Stone Cold rattlesnake rip-the-head-off-your-mother Steve Austin—didn't give The Rock a rematch.

Instead, he handed over his championship belt.

Huh?

Huh?!!?

Then he laid The Rock out with a Stunner.

Austin said he was going after bigger things—the World Wrestling Federation Heavyweight Championship, rather than the Intercontinental—but fans were still confused by Austin's outbreak of (relative) passivity.

The Rock's focus over the next few weeks would be on the Intercontinental title, which he would win and successfully defend (thanks to a disqualification) against Ken Shamrock at *WrestleMania XIV*. The Rock also spent considerable time battling Faarooq, the erstwhile leader of the Nation who was angered by his new popularity. The Rock's differences with Austin were not entirely forgotten, however, as he lost to Austin at *Royal Rumble* at the end of January.

Austin also stole the championship belt before McMahon could officially present it to The Rock: He threw it off a bridge into the river, then disappeared into the night.

McMahon called The Rock "the People's Champion." At first the term was something to be snickered at. But gradually, The Rock turned fans' attitudes around. They responded by making him one of the more popular wrestlers in the company.

In 1998, he and Mankind faced off for the Heavyweight Championship. By now, the fans were firmly in The Rock's corner, and he was butting heads with his onetime supporter Mr. McMahon, who had turned against him as his popularity increased.

At the end of the match, now-champion The Rock drank in the applause. But the audience suddenly fell silent as Mr. McMahon and his son Shane entered.

Most of the fans expected that Mr. McMahon would have some reason to take the title away, or that The Rock would lay out both of his nemeses. What they didn't expect was what actually happened: The Rock extended his hand, peacefully, and all three men celebrated his championship.

The Rock had gone from the People's Champion to the Corporate Champion.

Babyface to heel, inside of a second and a half.

Which made him perfect fodder for Steve Austin, who soon arrived to his trademark sound of breaking glass.

WRESTLEMANIA XV

The Rock continued to face off against Mankind, but the real showdown that was shaping up was Rock-Austin. Briefly relinquishing the title to Mankind, The Rock won it back at a Ladder match on *Raw* just in time to set up a title defense at *WrestleMania XV*.

Mr. McMahon wanted The Rock to win the match, and he set about doing so. First he declared it a No-Disqualification contest, depriving Austin of any hope that either dirty tricks or his friends could end the match prematurely, preserving his title. Then Mr. McMahon named Mankind as special referee. Given that Mankind had been fighting with The Rock and could hardly be expected to be neutral, this was a puzzling move by the chairman.

Things started looking up for The Rock just before the match, when injuries made it impossible for Mankind to make the opening bell. Emboldened, The Rock seized the initiative right away, trash talking Stone Cold as soon as Austin climbed in the ring. Austin objected, and the two began exchanging blows. They ended up brawling in the crowd for nearly ten minutes before the officials managed to get things under control and shepherd them back to the ring.

The No-Disqualification match helped The Rock early on, as he found a rope or cable on the floor and choked Austin with it. Nearly five minutes later, he threw Stone Cold down near one of the announcers' tables, chugged a bottle of water, and spit a mouthful on the challenger. Austin, infuriated, put The Rock through the table.

Though Austin was still the favorite, the audience gave The Rock one of the biggest ovations of the match midway through when he nearly pinned Stone Cold shortly after they returned to the ring. Boosted by the crowd, The Rock kept up the attack. When the match moved outside the ring, he used a steel chair to punish Austin and knocked him senseless. He yelled to the ref that Austin was unconscious and should be counted out. But that was like sounding a bugle in Austin's ear. Almost instantaneously, Stone Cold jumped up and began smacking The Rock around the ring.

The Rock rebounded. Fifteen minutes into the match, with Austin down in the corner, Mr. McMahon came into the ring to give The Rock a hand—or rather a foot, which he applied liberally to Austin's midsection.

Mankind appeared, kicking Mr. McMahon out of the ring and counting The Rock down and gone, after a Stunner laid him out.

Austin celebrated with a beer in the ring.

BACKLASH

The two were set for a rematch at the next Pay-Per-View, *Backlash*, held in Providence, Rhode Island, at the end of April.

One of the themes of this portion of their continuing story line had to do with the championship belt itself. Austin had had a new belt made to replace the World Wrestling Federation's version. It had a smoking skull on it (like the image on his vest) and was often referred to as "the smoking skull belt."

The Rock's interest in belts was even more physical. During the run-up to *Backlash*, he visited the bridge where Stone Cold had thrown The Rock's Intercontinental title into the water a year before. He and Austin got into it there, with The Rock tossing Stone Cold into the water.

The following week, The Rock brought a hearse into the arena, promising he'd be using it to bury Stone Cold. He proceeded to officiate at a funeral for the "biggest foul-mouthed, beer-swilling, finger-gesturing piece of monkey crap that has ever graced God's green earth."

The Rock didn't bury Stone Cold, but he did inter his belt—maybe an even bigger insult.

Rock thought he had inside information that Stone Cold wasn't showing up that night. But of course Austin did, driving a monster truck over The Rock's brand-new Lincoln and then the hearse before whooping The Rock inside and taking back the championship.

COMING BACK FOR MORE

Stone Cold beat The Rock at the Pay-Per-View, despite efforts by acting ref Shane McMahon to help his opponent.

Shane refused to count out The Rock early in the match. The bout continued as Mr. McMahon interrupted, attacking Shane with Austin's championship belt and inserting a real ref in his son's place.

Stone Cold retained his title by downing The Rock with a Stunner. Rock was probably the one who was stunned, given that he had been helped by his longtime nemesis. It wasn't the start of a great friendship, by any means, just a momentary diversion.

In the following weeks, The Rock's focus shifted to Shane, Tripe H, and other Superstars. But he and Stone Cold would go on to meet twice more at *WrestleMania*.

WRESTLEMANIA X-SEVEN

Austin and The Rock renewed their feud just before *WrestleMania X-Seven* in 2001. Austin had sustained a series of injuries but was still a tough opponent. The Rock was the champ for the sixth time, having beaten Kurt Angle at *No Way Out* in February 2001.

This installment of their feud started in the middle of March, after Stone Cold's wife, Debra, was made The Rock's manager by Mr. McMahon. Stone Cold told The Rock that he would hold him personally responsible if anything happened to her in the ring. Sure enough, after Kurt Angle put a vicious anklelock on her during a *Raw* match on March 12, Stone Cold put a Stunner on The Rock.

CROWD FAVORITE

Wrestling at the Houston Astrodome in his home state of Texas, Austin was a fan favorite. The Rock had a substantial portion of the crowd behind him as well and at several points drew even bigger cheers from the crowd. At twenty-eight, The Rock was at the top of the profession; this was his third *WrestleMania* main event in a row.

Stealing a page from The Rock's book at their last *Wrestle-Mania*, Austin began the fight before the bell had rung. It was another No-Disqualification match, and the pace was quick, despite the fact that Austin was wearing braces on both knees.

The Rock, looking faster and more athletic than ever before, nonetheless took the early action on the chin as the fight carried into the stands. Austin removed the padding from one of the turnbuckles to increase The Rock's pain and used the ring bell as a weapon. He also tossed the timekeeper out of his way while raging outside the ring.

The fight chased the commentators from their table as Stone Cold began pummeling The Rock. He punched, he slapped, he threw The Rock against the exposed turnbuckle.

Blood began flowing from The Rock's forehead. The crowd shifted, deciding it wanted Austin to win. And then The Rock rocketed from the corner, changing the momentum of the match. What was good for the challenger was good for the champ—The Rock threw Austin down with the bell, and it was Stone Cold's turn to bleed.

Outside the ring again, Austin managed to catapult The Rock into the ring post. Next he clocked him with a TV monitor. With the crowd chanting "Au-stin, Au-stin," he threw The Rock into the ring but couldn't get a pin.

Another reversal—The Rock got Stone Cold in a Sharpshooter. The two men crawled back and forth before Austin managed to touch the rope, ending the hold.

A minute later, after an exchange of fingers, Austin put The Rock into his own Sharpshooter. The Rock broke it with sheer strength. Within moments, Austin managed to nearly choke The Rock into submission. But the action was just getting going.

MR. McMAHON & AUSTIN

With the wrestlers continuing to punch each other in the center of the ring, Mr. McMahon walked out from the back and down to ringside. The Rock got the People's Elbow (an elbow drop to the chest) on Austin, succeeding with the move for one of the first times in their confrontations.

With Austin all but pinned, Mr. McMahon crawled into the ring and dragged The Rock off his opponent, extending the duel. The Rock chased Mr. McMahon around the ring, returning in time to get smacked with a Rock Bottom by Austin.

Austin called to Mr. McMahon and held The Rock up for

him as he smacked him with a chair. The crowd was unsure whom to root for, but when The Rock kicked out of a hold a few moments later, they cheered tentatively for the reigning champ.

When The Rock smashed Mr. McMahon in the corner minutes later, he cemented the fans' allegiance. Kickout after kickout, The Rock's backing grew. But Austin's popularity ran wide and deep, and when he got the pin after pounding The Rock with a chair, the arena exploded.

ENDING WITH A GRUDGE

The next time the two men faced each other was at *Wrestle-Mania XIX*, held at Safeco Field in Seattle in March 2003. It was a grudge match, held right before the headline title contest between Kurt Angle and Brock Lesnar.

Behind the scenes, Austin had been out of action for roughly nine months. During that time, The Rock had gotten in touch with his musical side, grabbing a guitar and singing about how much he hated Sacramento while performing there. That didn't go over well with the crowd. Nor did his mocking of Hulk Hogan, who had returned to WWE and was once again a fan favorite.

Unlike their earlier bouts, the one at *WrestleMania XIX* started with a stare down. Within a few seconds, the two ex-champs were back at it, mixing it up on the apron and the ramp to the locker room.

Stone Cold dominated the early minutes of the match. Then low shots by The Rock into Austin's knees gave him the momentum. Things moved more slowly than they had two years before, until a flurry by Austin in midmatch brought the crowd to its feet.

The Rock escaped and managed to apply a sharpshooter on Austin. Failing to get a submission or pin, The Rock kept coming, trying to break Austin's legs. Adding insult to injury, he grabbed the vest Stone Cold had thrown down near the ring and put it on.

The result was predictable: Austin's anger propelled him across the ring. Both men went down from the force of the collision. Austin got up first and continued pummeling The Rock as the fans' cheers became louder and louder.

The Rock rallied, bringing his own fans to their feet with a Stunner on Austin. Kickout followed kickout. With roughly sixteen minutes gone, fifty-four thousand people were on their feet. A People's Elbow missed . . . then scored. But The Rock couldn't get the pin.

Next, a Rock Bottom failed to put Austin away.

The crowd began chanting "Rock-y!"

A second Rock Bottom.

Same result.

The third time was the charm. The Rock had finally topped his nemesis.

After this match both men's careers took new turns, and they never again faced each other in the ring. But they had already been to the mountaintop—not once, not twice, but a magical three times.

EDGE & CHRISTIAN
VS. HARDYS
VS. DUDLEYS

Tables, ladders, chairs—volatile ingredients in a wrestling match. Put them together in the ring, and you know there's going to be trouble.

Put them together at *WrestleMania*, and you have one of the greatest Tag Team showdowns of all time—a three-way face-off of Edge & Christian, the Dudley Boys, and the Hardy Boys.

EDGE & CHRISTIAN

In the fall of 1999, tag team fans began focusing their attention on two up-and-coming teams, Edge & Christian, and Matt and Jeff Hardy, known together as the Hardy Boys (or Hardy Boyz, as it was often styled).

The two teams had a lot in common. They favored an athletic, high-flying style when in the ring. They seemed fearless, willing not just to inflict pain but to dish it out. Both teams had aligned with Gangrel, at different times, as part of the New Brood. And above all, both were talented and ambitious.

Like didn't attract like, however. Like attracted hate and confrontation. Egged on at times by the blond bimbos' irreverent sarcasm, the Hardys wished only evil things for Edge & Christian. Edge & Christian returned the sentiment.

The two teams were natural enemies, but they had another incentive to face off when the Terri Runnels Invitational Tournament was announced. The prize in the round-robin tourney was $100,000—and Terri Runnels, the cigar-smoking, P.M.S. (Pretty Mean Sister) Diva who would serve as the winners' manager. Runnels had mostly left the cigar-smoking gimmick behind with her earlier incarnation as Marlena, but even without it, she was smoking hot.

THE LADDER MATCH

Fighting for the girl predates wrestling as entertainment, and the cash prize seemed paltry by comparison.

To win the tourney, a team needed three victories over its opponents. This set up an epic series between the Hardy Boys and Edge & Christian that went not five matches, but six. Edge & Christian got the first two, then saw their chance to clinch slip away in a disqualification at the third match. The next two contests went to the Hardy Boys.

The deciding meeting was set for *No Mercy 1999*, held in Cleveland on October 17. As part of the gimmick, the $100,000 prize was hoisted above the center of the ring. The match would be won when one team retrieved the money using a ladder.

It's not exactly clear where the idea of a Ladder match originated. Some sources claim that it began in Canada in the 1970s, but given the spotty records of early wrestling, it's very possible it was around much earlier. It has, however, often been associated with Canadians, even in the United States—Bret Hart won a World Wrestling Federation title in one in 1992.

The 1990s and early 2000s saw several Ladder matches. A few months before *No Mercy*, Shane McMahon and Mr. McMahon had defeated Stone Cold Steve Austin in a Ladder match at *King of the Ring*. But the Christian & Edge–Hardy Boys showdown appears to have been the first Ladder match between tag teams at a major event.

NO MERCY

Accompanied by Gangrel, the Hardy Boys were introduced as the New Brood at the match. There was a good deal of action outside the ring from the start, with the ladders at one point flying nearly as high as the wrestlers. Inside the ring, team member after team member tried to climb up, only to be toppled.

During the middle of the match, the wrestlers performed their moves off the ladders. Dropkicks, suplexes, Powerbombs, super bombs—most of the teams' signature moves were altered to include a ladder somehow. As in most Ladder matches, the ladders were also used as everything from battering rams to catapults.

The acrobatic spots the wrestlers performed impressed the crowd so much it didn't take sides for most of the match. The fans counted with Christian & Edge as they sandwiched and beat Jeff Hardy with one of the ladders, then applauded as all four wrestlers crashed to the canvas as both ladders toppled.

Matt Hardy finally set up a ladder and managed to grab

the money and jump to the mat, winning the tourney for the Boys.

TOWARD A THREESOME

It was the end of the event, but not the conflict between the Hardy Boys and Christian & Edge, who continued to come up against each other in Tag Team fights over the next year. Matt and Jeff left the Brood. When they saved Lita from a beating by Essa Rios, she joined them. They became Team Xtreme, and their new member's sex appeal made them even more popular with the fans.

Then another tag team joined the rumble for the top spot: the Dudleys. If two times two was more than four, three times two was well into double digits.

DUDLEY BOYS

The Dudley Boys were members of the larger Dudley family. Brother Ray and Brother D-Von worked as a tag team in WWE after coming over from Extreme Championship Wrestling in 1999. (At the time, ECW and WWE were separate companies.)

Brother Ray—or Bubba Ray—was the "nerd" brother, wearing thick taped glasses and talking with a pronounced stutter. (The stutter tended to disappear when he was very excited, a fact the crowd was probably thankful for.) To get his tongue working correctly, D-Von slapped his back, sending the words spitting into the audience.

The Dudleys had made a name for themselves in ECW by bringing tables into the ring and using them in the act. Usually their opponents ended up going through them, often thanks to the brothers' signature move, the Dudley Death

Drop, or 3D as it was often called. Typically, brother D-Von would grab an opponent and toss him in a flapjack throw; Ray would then grab the opponent and execute an elevated cutter. With the opponent temporarily dazed, the Dudleys would then send him through the table, setting up the final pin.

A variation called for the opponents' woman manager to be sent through the table (riding down on Bubba's lap). The move gave him an orgasmic high, sending him into a trance. The Dudleys had no respect for age or beauty: They tormented eighty-year-old Mae Young; they crashed Lita.

Fans loved it.

LADDERS AT *WRESTLEMANIA*

The three tag teams exchanged bad wishes over the course of the year, and their multifaceted rivalry helped bring attention to a category often overlooked.

Edge & Christian beat the Hardy Boys at *Survivor Series 1999* and *No Way Out 2000*, setting themselves up for a three-way tussle for the tag team belt at *WrestleMania XVI* on April 2.

In the days leading up to the match, Edge & Christian interrupted the Hardys during an interview; the Hardys returned the favor. Edge & Christian also took every opportunity to mock the Dudleys, who gave back as g-g-g-good as they could.

Harking back to the standout tournament match between Edge & Christian and the Hardys, the championship meet was set up as a Ladder match. The fight went on for more than twenty minutes, with as much action outside the ring as in it. Flinging and flying around, the contestants abused their own bodies as badly as they did their opponents'.

Not quite halfway through the match, Bubba wore one of the ladders, Three Stooges–style, turning it into a weapon and decking everyone in sight. The advantage was short-lived. A cross-body by Christian from the top of a ladder took out Bubba and one of the Hardys, and things continued to accelerate out of control. Dive after dive, the contestants fell from one ladder or another to the canvas.

The audience was along for the ride, cheering and ahhing with each leap and scamper. A 3D on Edge put the Dudleys in position to win, but rather than climbing for their championship belts, the two wrestlers hopped out of the ring and grabbed tables from under the mat.

The crowd grew silent as the Dudleys made a bridge from ladders and a table in the center of ring. The Hardys were Powerbombed through two tables, one inside, one outside the ring.

All that separated the Dudleys from the title were Christian & Edge — and their own engineering skills, as they continued to arrange their table/ladder complex, adding twelve-foot ladders and tables out in the runway area.

The Hardys had been knocked down, not out. Jeff Hardy reappeared, somersaulting onto Bubba, who flew through the table outside the ring. Christian and Matt Hardy, moving in slow motion, climbed the ladders in the ring and fought it out on the table in between, until Edge rose from the mangled knot he'd lain in for nearly five minutes and tumbled Hardy for the victory.

TLC

The match was dubbed one of the finest of the year by many fans, who naturally demanded a rematch. Another super-showdown among the three tag teams was planned for *SummerSlam* in Raleigh, North Carolina, on August 27, 2000.

The *SummerSlam* match was the first TLC contest, standing not for tender loving care but tables, ladders, and chairs, all of which were legal instruments of construction and destruction in the ring.

By this time, Edge & Christian had honed their mocking sarcasm into a fine art, going so far as to lampoon their opponents with the help of dwarfs, who posed with them in a thirty-seven-second mock homage tableau before the match.

Odd, but funny.

The wrestlers' goal in the match was to snare the championship belts hung above the stage, but the real spotlight was on the spots and stunts in, around, and over the ring.

In Dudley parlance, an opponent who was sent through a table was "looking for wood," a reference to the material the tabletop was made of. Everyone here was looking for wood, and they got it.

Following a number of chair shots and other diversions, Bubba was sent through a stack of two tables from near the top of a ladder twelve (or twenty, depending on whose commentary you trust) feet high.

"Carnage!" shouted one of the announcers.

Truer words were rarely uttered at a wrestling match. Every conceivable spot, and a few that weren't conceivable, was tried in combination with the chairs, ladders, and tables as the wrestlers played "top this" with each other's bodies.

LITA'S SAVE

As the last two standing, Edge & Christian were reaching for the belts when Lita ran in and dumped them, preserving the victory for . . .

The Hardy Boys, in theory, since Lita was their manager and ally. And as Carolina boys, they were the hometown favorites. But D-Von got up as well and raced Jeff Hardy for the belt. Dangling over the center of the ring, they kicked and hissed at each other until D-Von fell away.

The delay allowed Edge & Christian to rebound. Swatting Jeff to the mat, Edge & Christian climbed the ladder and took the trophies.

The match was enormously popular, thanks to the sheer violence of the action. There have been other TLC matches since, but this one continues to rate as arguably the best, so packed with spots that it's impossible to describe. You have to watch it—several times.

MASKING THEIR EMOTIONS

Christian & Edge continued to clash with the Hardy Boys, losing to them in a Cage match at *Unforgiven* later in the year. This set up the teams for a complicated story line involving a team championship exchange tournament, a kind of wrestle-off that extended over several weeks.

Christian & Edge were disqualified from the tourney early on, meaning they no longer had a chance to take the championship. Deciding all was not lost, they donned masks and wrestled as Los Conquistadors, a (supposedly) Mexican team of *luchadores*.

They did very well, and in fact took the championship at

No Mercy in October 2000, defeating the Hardys. Their disguises weren't perfect, and the pair couldn't resist pulling some of their trademark satire, but they stayed masked, and their identities remained a secret.

So how would Christian & Edge get the title?

Easy. They'd just beat Los Conquistadors, whom they faced the next night on *Raw*. The pair hired a duo of rookies to don the masks and got ready to cash in.

The rookies put up a hell of a good show.

Too good, in fact. They defeated their employers handily, retaining the title.

Or winning it back, since when they pulled off their masks, Los Conquistadors revealed themselves as the Hardy Boys. They'd switched places with the rookies before the match.

A WILLINGNESS TO HURT

The high-flying acrobatic wrestling the three teams demonstrated was the biggest attraction in this showdown. The jumps seemed life threatening, and in fact at least one journalist felt moved to write an editorial advising them to "cool it" before they got hurt.

Christian & Edge joined Kurt Angle to form Team ECK and then Team Reck (with Rhyno). They helped the Hardy Boys defeat the Dudleys, then took the title for themselves in early 2001.

A final three-way TLC at *WrestleMania X-Seven* reprised the earlier match. The novelty may have been gone, but the bruises were just as real. With help from Rhyno, Christian & Edge took their seventh and final tag team title.

The match featured an incredible somersaulting dive by

Jeff Hardy off a twelve-foot ladder outside the ring into a table—and onto Rhyno and Spike. Edge then spiked Jeff as he hung from the belt above the ring; Bubba and Matt Hardy did a double smash onto the tables before Edge managed to grab the championship belt and end the match.

The Hardy Boys, the Dudleys, and Christian & Edge continued their high-octane showdowns into 2002, until the Hardy Boys and the Dudleys split up, the members going solo. The Dudleys, Matt and Jeff Hardy, and Christian were all out of WWE by 2005, leaving Edge the last one standing—a honor in and of itself given the brutality of the matches they had all endured. The Hardys have since returned, giving TLC aficionados something to hope for.

CHRIS JERICHO VS. STEPHANIE McMAHON VS. TRIPLE H

They say all is fair in love and war. But what happens when love turns to war?

Is there no end to the amount of violence a couple can do to each other?

Pretty much, if the case of Triple H and Stephanie McMahon's troubled marriage is any proof. Of course, the conflict was aided and abetted by Chris Jericho, who is no one's idea of an ideal marriage counselor.

NOTHIN' BUT A TRASH BAG HO

The three-way tangle with Jericho, Triple H, and Stephanie came during the period when Triple H was aligned with the McMahon family, largely because of his (then fictional) marriage to Stephanie, who was the promotion's general manager.

Triple H had cleaned up his image, cutting his hair, donning tight leather trunks, and sporting an iron cross. Jericho, who'd been in the company about eight or nine months, had taken to calling himself Y2J, capitalizing on the hype about the so-called millennium, or Y2K, bug. (There was a widespread belief that computers and other electronic devices would fail when the calendar changed at the end of 1999. The fear had been seeded by legitimate concerns about obsolescent computer programs, but was clearly overhyped.)

The showdown began as a disagreement between Jericho and Stephanie on the April 13, 2000, *SmackDown!* show, when Jericho mistook her for a prostitute. He apologized, but after a nasty tangle with DX in a Handicap match later in the show, Jericho claimed that she had controlled the proceedings as a way of avenging the slight. He unleashed a string of vitriol in her direction, hurling epithets that included "trash bag ho."

The battle was on.

THE TITLE CHANGE THAT WASN'T

Triple H, then the World Wrestling Federation champion, set out to avenge his wife's honor the following week on *Raw* (at this point, the shows did not have separate Superstars). He and Jericho set up a match to settle their differences. While the bout was not supposed to be for the title, after pressure from Jericho the championship was put on the line. A conflict between referee Earl Hebner and Triple H led Hebner to quick-count a pin on the champion at the match, giving the title to Jericho.

Triple H was livid. Seeking to force Hebner to reverse the decision, Triple H first threatened and then bribed Hebner to declare a DQ in his favor. The bribe was simple: If Hebner reversed the decision, Triple H would never abuse him again while he was in the company.

Yes, you figured it out: Hebner reversed the decision and was immediately fired and pummeled. Triple H got the title back, with all record of the change erased.

FULLY LOADED 2000

Tempers within the trio continued to flare, with Jericho attacking Triple H and trash mouthing his wife. Finally, the two men had it out at the July 23, 2000, Pay-Per-View *Fully Loaded*, fighting in a Last-Man-Standing match.

Despite his smaller size, Jericho began as the aggressor, sending a flurry of punches into his antagonist. Within minutes, he was zipping around the ring, landing a leaping kick to his opponent's face and threatening to run away with the match on mere adrenaline.

Forced outside the ropes, Triple H found new energy after a kiss from his wife. Zeroing in on Jericho's barely healed ribs, Triple H took over the middle of the match. He couldn't manage a pin, and as his momentum stalled, Jericho rebounded. Bleeding from a chair smash to the face, Triple H staggered as Jericho once again unleashed a flurry of fists. After the battle moved to the apron, both men laid each other out; both rose after an eight count and staggered back to the ring. (In a Last-Man-Standing match, a wrestler must rise before a ten count or be deemed out.)

Jericho tried his Walls of Jericho hold to win a submission. Groaning with pain but refusing to give up, Triple H crawled to the rope to win a release. But the referee wouldn't make Jericho break the hold, and as Jericho pulled him back toward the middle of the ring, Stephanie climbed in and confronted Jericho.

Jericho dropped Triple H and put *her* in the hold—and in the process made the always fatal mistake of turning his back on Triple H. The battle went outside the ropes again: This time, Triple H pulled a sledgehammer from beneath the ring and began waling on Jericho.

Or would have, had he not hit the ring post instead.

The smash was so intense, Triple H was himself stunned. Jericho, depleted, fought him over to the tables. The two wrestlers crashed downward, wiping out various hardware and themselves.

Triple H managed to rise at the ref's ten count, claiming the win—and then promptly collapsed.

SECOND PHASE

Tempers cooled a bit after *Fully Loaded*, but this was primarily due to the fact that the protagonists had more pressing business. Roughly a year later, Jericho and Stephanie were back at it almost full-time.

Trash talking by Jericho had characterized the first phase of the story line; it returned now with a vengeance. Jericho taunted Stephanie unmercifully.

When Stephanie was about to celebrate her birthday, Jericho asked, "How old are you going to be? Thirty-seven? Thirty-eight?"

"Twenty-five," answered Stephanie.

"No, I asked how old you were going to be, not how many men you've slept with this week."

The audience quickly picked up on the slut charges, and during at least one show chanted "ho, ho" as Jericho laced into her.

"For you, *SummerSlam* is a quickie on a hot August night," claimed Jericho, before going on to accuse her of sleeping with three-quarters of the locker room . . . and the lighting crew, and just about everyone else in the building.

The attack was relentless. Jericho brought out *Planet of the Apes* look-alikes, then slammed her with cream pie, setting up a camera shot that suggested something more X-rated.

TRIPLE H OUT

And where was her husband all this time?

Triple H had been injured in a Tag Team battle with, ironically, Jericho on *Raw* in May. Working with Stone Cold Steve Austin against Jericho and Chris Benoit, Triple H had torn a quadriceps muscle so severely it needed to be surgically repaired. He would not return to action until the following January.

The Jericho-Stephanie conflict was just one in a series of clashes between and among wrestlers and the McMahons, and Stephanie had several motivations for her actions. But so hot was Stephanie's hatred that she probably would have backed the devil himself against Jericho.

So how can we explain that it was *Jericho* who defended her from *Triple H* a few months later?

And became her ally at *WrestleMania*, no less?

TURNAROUND

It all happened in February, soon after Triple H's return to the ring.

During an interview with Jim Ross, Stephanie realized that her marriage wasn't going well. Desperate to somehow patch things up, she came up with the idea of renewing her wedding vows. Triple H was initially reluctant . . . until Stephanie blurted out that she was pregnant.

At first apprehensive, Triple H reacted with joy, hugging his wife and agreeing to the ceremony.

But, alas, Stephanie was *not* pregnant, a fact that most in the audience suspected/knew from the start and that Triple H soon came to find out. He waited, however, until the ceremony to denounce her, where he not only completed the marriage break but turned on her father as well, ending the McMahon-Helmsley alliance.

"Tonight I see you not as my loving wife," he told her on the February 11, 2002, *Raw*, "not as the mother of my child . . . but for what you truly are . . . a no-good lying bitch."

The story turned into a rift on the marriage breakup, evoking memories of the movie *War of the Roses*. The couple did unspeakable (but viewable) things to each other. Triple H cut Stephanie's prize Corvette in half; Stephanie tormented Lucy, his adorably ugly bulldog.

LUCY & JERICHO

As her marriage was breaking up, World Wrestling Federation champion Jericho approached Stephanie and apologized for having said so many nasty things about her the previous year. The two eventually came to a business agreement where they would work together; Jericho wanted to remain champion, and Stephanie needed a strong wrestler to help her franchise and position.

Stephanie's original plan had been to push Kurt Angle and deprive Triple H of a shot at the championship. But this was foiled by Angle's loss to Triple H at *No Way Out*, so the alignment with Jericho made sense.

Meanwhile, to spite her soon to be ex-husband, Stephanie got a judge to grant her custody of Lucy. She really didn't like the dog, but getting custody was just one way of getting back at him.

When Jericho accidentally ran over the dog, Stephanie freaked. She knew Triple H would blame her for killing the dog.

She was right. He chased her around the ring, catching her by the hair and preparing to thrash her.

"I don't know what's going to happen," declared J.R., "but whatever it is, this woman deserves it."

As Triple H was about to apply a Pedigree, slamming her to the mat, Jericho ran in and hit his knee with a sledgehammer.

JERICHO–TRIPLE H

The attack came right before *WrestleMania* X8, putting the icing on the buildup for the two men's championship match. The fans had changed sides, and were now behind Triple H and against Jericho. Or perhaps more accurately, the audience loathed Stephanie and anything remotely connected to her.

The match began with Triple H working on Jericho's knee, a turnaround from the audience's expectations. With Jericho in a figure four, Stephanie came to ringside and raked her fingernails across Triple H's eyes, forcing him to break the hold. Triple H then grabbed her by the hair and hauled her into the ring.

The distractions gave Jericho an opening, and he took control of the match, dominating until Triple H managed to kick him into the ring post. From there on, the match seesawed back and forth. Jericho kicked out of a nasty spinebuster and Triple H crashed through an announcer's table. Outside the ring, Jericho reversed a Pedigree into a back drop so devastating that the floor of the arena shook. But he couldn't get a pin or a submission after dragging Triple H back into the ring.

Referee Earl Hebner spent a good portion of the match trying to keep Stephanie from interfering. It was a largely futile effort. But when she got by the ref one too many times, Triple H used a Pedigree to smash her to the canvas, temporarily knocking her out.

Jericho clocked Triple H, then went to cover for the pin. With Hebner attending to Stephanie, he couldn't get the count. Frustrated, Jericho put Triple H into a Pedigree, hoping to humiliate his opponent by using his own closing move against him. Triple H reversed it, and the two wrestlers began a furious exchange that ended with a Pedigree on Jericho that gave Triple H the championship.

YOU'RE OUT

The three-way dispute ended on *Raw* right after the *Wrestle-Mania* match, when Triple H beat Stephanie and Jericho in a Stipulation match—the stipulation being that if Triple H won, Stephanie was out forever.

Triple H did win, and Stephanie was out . . . though not quite forever. But that's a different story.

JOHN CENA
VS. JBL

I t's easy to get riled up when a rich braggart starts throwing his weight around. But when that braggart starts acting like a big-shot politician to boot, there'll be hell to pay.

John "Bradshaw" Layfield, better known as JBL, learned that lesson when he faced John Cena in their war before, after, and during *WrestleMania 21*.

Then again, given JBL's nature, one might argue that no lesson was learned at all.

JBL

Reminiscent of J. R. Ewing, the *Dallas* patriarch, JBL is a lavish-spending Texan who thought the world revolved around him.

After taking the WWE Championship title in a match against Eddie Guerrero at *Judgment Day 2004*, he began gathering a group of wrestlers around him who would be called the cabinet, a nod toward his politician-style reign.

Among the cabinet's most prominent members were Orlando Jordan, his chief of staff; Amy Weber, his image consultant; and the Basham Brothers (Doug and Danny Basham).

By the time JBL squared off with John Cena, he had reigned about nine months, the longest anyone had held the title in a decade.

SMACK DOWN ON *SMACKDOWN!*

The conflict between Cena and JBL had its seeds in a *Royal Rumble* battle in January 2005, when Cena and Dave "the Animal" Batista dueled in an unprecedented sudden-death finish to the rumble. By winning, Batista earned the right to challenge a champion, and he would eventually face off against Triple H at *WrestleMania* for the World Heavyweight title.

Meanwhile, Cena entered a *SmackDown!* contenders' tournament, trying to get his own crack at the WWE Championship (a different title) held by JBL. But in doing so, he found himself going up against Orlando Jordan, a member of JBL's cabinet.

JBL dissed Cena on *Raw*, saying he wasn't WWE Champion material. "He has no quality, no class," said JBL, using words that he would repeat over and over. "He should not represent WWE."

Cena liked this not one bit and set out to shut JBL's big mouth, bouncing him and Jordan from the ring moments after JBL's bragging.

Cena defeated Jordan the next week and began working his way through the other contenders. JBL had more important matters to contend with—Big Show was making a push for his title. And there was Batista, at this point a *Raw* regular who looked like he might "invade" *SmackDown!* in an effort to challenge JBL himself. But Cena got JBL's attention at the end of February when he broke up JBL's "celebration of excellence," a self-aggrandizing party commemorating JBL's reign as champ. At the height of the party, Cena smashed a painting of JBL over the champion's head, framing the conflict between them.

BUILDUP

The showdown continued to build toward *WrestleMania 21*. Cena bad-mouthed JBL; JBL helped Orlando Jordan in a match against Cena. At *No Way Out* near the end of February 2005, Cena won the contenders' tournament final, besting Kurt Angle. JBL beat Big Show in a Barbed-Wire Steel Cage match, guaranteeing the showdown.

With the title contest now set, JBL unleashed all of his rhetoric on Cena, saying he was white trash with no hope of carrying the title properly. Cena was a thug—a play on Cena's *Thuganomics* theme—and didn't deserve to wear the championship belt.

Unlike JBL, of course, who practiced advanced economics, making him class and money personified.

Cena seethed and called his opponent WWE's longest-running bitch, rather than champ.

Cena was popular with the crowd; on several shows when JBL came onstage, fans spontaneously erupted with chants for Cena. While the two wrestlers threatened each other, an edict from Theodore Long, the *SmackDown!* GM, stipulated that Cena would lose his shot at the title if they came to blows. JBL even had Cena arrested for vandalism—Cena painted "JBL sucks" on his limo—but Cena managed to keep himself from hitting him.

WRESTLEMANIA

JBL arrived at *WrestleMania 21* in a steer-horn-adorned stretch limo, complete with a police escort. He tried winning over the crowd by showering them with money . . . printed with his name, of course.

The logo read "In JBL We Trust." Most of the crowd didn't.

Cena, by contrast, walked out in an oversized Chain Gang Soldier basketball T over jean shorts. He was the cool white rapper come to slay the titan of finance.

JBL was considerably larger than Cena. The weight mismatch was in the neighborhood of fifty pounds, with about five inches of height in JBL's favor. The height difference was immediately apparent, as the wrestlers locked up and began dancing back and forth in the ring.

The first half of the match was all JBL, with Cena absorbing various punishments. JBL knocked him down, twisted his head in the ropes, kicked him, choked him—but couldn't get a submission or pin.

Punch-drunk, Cena flailed at the champion, desperate just to remain on his feet. Finally, Cena managed to reverse a chokehold and slammed JBL to the mat. JBL began to tire, and the tide slowly turned.

When the action moved outside the ring, JBL tried to retake control with a neckbreaker. It didn't work. Dragging his opponent inside the ring, he tried using a suplex to set up the pin, but failed. Cena turned back a scoop slam but was too wiped out to cover.

As both men staggered to their feet, Cena suddenly caught fire. Throwing JBL over his shoulder, he began a run that climaxed with an F-U and a pin for the belt.

THE TITLE

The WWE Championship title belt and its appearance became a sidebar in the story line. Cena had a new belt designed, replacing the one JBL had worn.

The belt became the literal as well as figurative focus over the next few weeks, as the two wrestlers continued their war of words. JBL held on to the old title, carrying it around, proclaiming that the title should not be desecrated by the spinner design that Cena favored . . . and that, since he had the old one, he was still the "real" title holder.

Although JBL wanted a rematch, he had neglected to put a rematch clause in the fight contract and had to win his way into one. It took a four-way contenders' brawl on the April 28 *SmackDown!* for him to get his shot; he defeated Kurt Angle as well as Big Show and Booker T to set up the match at *Judgment Day*, May 1, 2005.

"I QUIT"

The *Judgment Day* meeting was to be decided *only* when one of the wrestlers said, "I quit," guaranteeing that the loser would be humiliated.

JBL took to the ring amid a chant for Cena. In contrast to his no-frills walk-in at *WrestleMania*, Cena entered the arena on the flatbed of a fuming tractor-trailer, a DJ gunning up his rap entrance theme. Walking across the roof of JBL's limo, Cena kicked off JBL's trademark steer horns before confronting JBL in the ring.

This match started faster than the previous one, with Cena using his speed to negate JBL's size advantage. JBL once more took control in the middle of the match, trying to turn it into a battle of attrition. Pushing Cena against the canvas—pins were meaningless—he punched his face again and again but drew barely a peep from his opponent.

Cena's persistence helped him take the fight outside the ring, where he used the steel steps to shake some of JBL's resolve. The two wrestlers were soon over the barrier into the edge of the crowd. Skulls met concrete as they took each other to the floor.

JBL dragged Cena to the Spanish announcer's table, grabbed a mike, and demanded that Cena say "I quit." Cena answered with a flurry of punches.

JBL pulled a belt off the timekeeper and used it to choke Cena on the ring post. Cena released himself out of the hold, then threw JBL through a table as the crowd cheered.

The match was far from over. A chair shot by JBL sent blood spraying from Cena's face. Punch-drunk, Cena flailed like a fish out of water. JBL began kicking him in time to the chant of "Ce-na" from the crowd—but couldn't get him to say he quit. Not even a chokehold with Cena's own chain could get him to give up.

Cena won release from the hold with a low blow, technically legal under the rules. But he was a rag doll in JBL's hands—until JBL called him a "punk-ass bitch."

Fist, Clothesline, headbutt, F-U: Cena brought everything he had left. Dazed, JBL started to leave the arena. Cena slammed him onto the hood of his limo, then was slammed himself by a neckbreaker that left a massive dent in the hood. JBL dragged him to some electrical equipment, tore out a wire, and once again tried choking him into submission.

"Come on, Cena," said the ref. "You wanna quit?"

"Hell noooooo!" managed Cena, working his fingers beneath the noose and breaking JBL's grip. He reversed the hold and sent JBL face-first through a television set.

Cena threw JBL into the limo through a window   without opening it. Glass flew everywhere. The wrestlers ended up on top of the car, where a Cena suplex stunned them both.

JBL rolled to the floor and tried to escape into the limo. Cena bounced him off the open door, then broke the door off and bashed it into the hood. JBL had enough left for one more flurry of punches as the fight moved to Cena's flatbed. Knocking Cena senseless, he tried one more time to choke Cena, this time using wire from the DJ setup on the truck. Cena grabbed the mike and battered JBL with it, knocking him off the speaker where he'd climbed onto a table.

Cena pulled one of the exhaust pipes off the truck and went after JBL with it.

"You wanna fight? I'm gonna fight!" said Cena, wielding the pipe.

JBL grabbed the mike.

"Son, I quit. I quit."

Blood in his eyes, barely aware of where he was, Cena let the ref hold his arm up, signifying victory.

Then he ran into JBL with the pipe anyway, sending him through a glass light display.

A CELEBRATED QUITTER

Humiliated, JBL was taunted over the next several weeks. Cena called him "the most celebrated quitter in WWE history," playing on JBL's old bragging line about being champ.

Except for some trash talking, the showdown between Cena and JBL had pretty much run its course; Cena moved over to *Raw* at the beginning of June. JBL stayed in *Smack-Down!* beginning a campaign against ECW before tangling with Batista.

14

RANDY ORTON
VS. UNDERTAKER

Whom do you send to kill a legend?
A legend killer, of course. But what happens if the legend is already dead?

UNDEAD AND UNBEATEN

Few streaks in recent wrestling history are as famous as Undertaker's victories at *WrestleMania*. At the beginning of 2005, the unbroken string had reached 12–0.

Undertaker would be considered a legend even without the streak, but given that *WrestleMania* is the highlight of the sports entertainment year, it is an extra set of exclamation marks.

It was also an open invitation to any wrestler wanting to prove himself. Young wrestlers looking for a ticket to fame eyed Undertaker the way a kid in the Old West looked at an aging gunfighter—a quick ticket to the top of the heap.

Or a one-way ride to Boot Hill, though brash newcomers rarely consider that.

RANDY ORTON

Randy Orton was both brash and a relative newcomer to WWE in 2005 when he set his sights on Undertaker, but the challenge made a great deal of sense.

He'd been in the company for roughly two years, earning his spurs as a member of Evolution, a faction led by Triple H and Ric Flair. And in a sense he'd been involved in the wrestling world his whole life. His father was "Cowboy" Bob Orton, a hall of famer who starred in the 1970s and early 1980s, most notably with the National Wrestling Association (NWA) and World Wrestling Federation. Bob Orton's father, Bob Sr.—Randy's grandfather—was himself a championship wrestler, wrestling under his own name and as Big O in a number of promotions during the 1950s and 1960s. That family connection would prove important as the showdown unfolded.

In 2003, Randy surprised a number of established wrestlers with upset victories, upending Shawn Michaels among others. His wins earned him the nickname "Legend Killer." Then in 2004, he became WWE's youngest World Heavyweight Champion ever, taking the title at the tender age of twenty-four.

The win sowed the seeds of his destruction. The other members of Evolution were jealous, and when conflict ensued, Orton found himself bested by faction leader Triple H, who used his experience as well as his position to put the upstart in his place.

The only place Orton wanted to be was in the wrestling penthouse. He decided the best way to get there was to set his sights beyond Triple H, to the one wrestler everyone in the company feared: Undertaker.

THE BEGINNING

Orton announced that he was going after Undertaker at the end of February 2005. His bravado couldn't completely hide the fact that, at least at first, he was intimidated by the Dead Man.

Not that he'd ever admit it. He regularly dished out an RKO—a jumping cutter, his finishing move—to anyone who didn't say he was going to win, or who showed the slightest doubt about the outcome. Among his victims was his girl-friend, Stacy Keibler, who he claimed had hesitated before showing her support.

A week before *WrestleMania 21*, Orton stood in the middle of the ring on *Raw* and began enunciating the reasons he would top Undertaker. Suddenly, flames shot from the ring posts. He might be brash, but he was no fool; he decided to get while the getting was good.

But when his father, "Cowboy" Bob Orton, joined him, Randy found a new store of courage. Here was a chance to combine the wisdom of age with the energy of youth. They'd be an unstoppable team.

Meanwhile, Undertaker was coldly confident that he would prevail. The two wrestlers were appearing on different shows—Orton on *Raw*, Undertaker on *SmackDown!*—and, until a few days before *WrestleMania*, had met only once, and then for just a few minutes to sign a contract for the match. Rather than signing, Orton smacked Undertaker in the face, then raced away before the Dead Man could take revenge.

On the last *SmackDown!* show before the Pay-Per-View, "Cowboy" Bob Orton showed up to speak to Undertaker. The senior Orton told Undertaker that his son had made a big mistake, letting his mouth do his thinking for him, and was now in over his head. Cowboy Bob begged for mercy.

Undertaker didn't look particularly moved, but that was irrelevant, since all Bob Orton had come to do was set him up for an attack by his son. Randy rushed the ring, dispatched Undertaker with a surprise RKO, and the two Ortons retreated, believing they had just taken the psychological advantage going into the match.

WRESTLEMANIA 21

At *WrestleMania*, Undertaker entered the ring with his usual flair, floating behind a procession of torch-carrying Druids as smoke and mist rose to the toll of his unearthly bell.

The match started with Randy Orton dancing around his larger opponent. Randy paused to slap Undertaker in the face as a sign of disrespect, maybe hoping to prove that he hadn't been intimidated. This only angered Undertaker, who began aggressively pursuing him around the ring. Orton managed to jump over Undertaker twice, but a vicious right hook from the Dead Man took him to the canvas.

Orton got up holding his jaw. Within seconds, he wasn't holding anything; in fact, the ropes were holding him as Undertaker slammed against his body again and again.

A rally by Orton set up a try at the RKO, but Undertaker merely flicked him out of the ring. Then a missed shot by Undertaker gave Orton an opening, and the match turned into a slugfest as the challenger attempted to pound Undertaker back into his coffin.

That strategy may have been ill-advised against a wrestler known for his ability to take punishment. A cheer of "Randy sucks!" went up from the crowd at the Staples Center in L.A. Undertaker began returning punch for punch.

After a dragon sleeper knocked Orton's breath from his body, the two wrestlers exchanged near pins and crushing holds. Orton got Undertaker in the corner and climbed the ropes to lash fists at his face. Undertaker took the punishment, then picked up Orton and carried him to center ring, trying to set up a Tombstone Piledriver for a finish. Before he could set it up, he was on the canvas himself—"Cowboy" Bob Orton had rushed into the ring to help his son.

Undertaker kicked out just before three. Now there was hell to pay.

A kick to Cowboy Bob's face sent him to the apron floor. Undertaker turned on Randy for a chokeslam but was surprised by an RKO. He barely escaped a pin. Orton stole Undertaker's finish—throat slash, Tombstone, and all—and the crowd jumped to its feet, suspecting, fearing, hoping the end of the streak.

Hoping?

Well no, probably not.

Undertaker reversed Randy's move into his own Tombstone and ended the match with a decisive pin.

BACK AT IT

That June, both men met on *SmackDown!* and tempers flared once again.

Orton began the feud by spearing Undertaker at the end of a match between the Dead Man and JBL. Orton was out for revenge, angered by having been drafted to *SmackDown!* from *Raw*, and just plain ornery.

The next week, Orton talked about wanting a rematch with Undertaker under *his* terms but fled when Undertaker's gong warned of his nemesis's approach.

As it turned out, the two had to wait until July to get it on.

Randy Orton once more did a run-in on Undertaker and JBL, costing Undertaker a contender's slot for the Heavyweight Championship title. The next week, Orton laid out his plans to take Undertaker at *SummerSlam*, the same Pay-Per-View that had brought him the world title the previous August.

Orton tuned up for the match with a replay of his previous year's victory, facing Chris Benoit on *SmackDown!* August 18, 2005. After he beat Benoit, Undertaker came into the ring and showed just how much he enjoyed being mocked by chokeslamming Randy into the canvas.

SUMMERSLAM

Orton started the *SummerSlam* match with a counterintuitive move, ducking out of the ring and walking around the apron area. He wanted to set his own pace, but this didn't stop him from getting slapped to the floor of the ring when he came back.

The first few minutes were mostly Undertaker's. A foot to the face put Orton in his place on the mat, but several attempts at a pin failed. Undertaker continued to attack Orton's recently repaired shoulder, using his size and strength to lever his opponent into the canvas. A series of haymakers failed to stop Orton, and Undertaker continued to hold the momentum, getting a near fall as he pressed home a relentless attack.

Slipping against the ropes, Orton looked out of it, little more than a punching bag. Finally, he managed to duck as Undertaker came at him leg first, and the momentum began to shift. Randy jumped on Undertaker's left leg as he was momentarily tangled in the ropes. Hobbled, Undertaker became a barely moving target for Orton's boot.

Undertaker managed to reverse a leglock, turning the tide back against Orton. He kicked at Orton's left kneecap, hobbling him as well, and then launched him out of the ring.

Dazed, Orton barely escaped a pin. Undertaker hoisted Orton to his shoulder and threw him against the corner for a snake-eyes thrust. Orton rebounded with a flying leap, putting his boot into Undertaker's face and laying him across the canvas.

Undertaker rose, and the pair began a series of broken Tombstones, each reversing the other's hold until Orton ended the series with a neckbreaker. Undertaker just barely beat the count, then caught Orton as he flew in from the top of the ropes. Chokeslamming his opponent to the canvas, he prepared to finish him.

Just then, a "fan" ran into the ring, distracting everyone. By the time security pulled him out, Orton had recovered— though he was smart enough to play possum.

Distraction over, Undertaker sauntered to Orton for the pin.

Surprise!

Orton shocked Undertaker, rebounding from the canvas to slap on an RKO. He hung on for the victory.

The fan turned out to be Orton's dad, Cowboy Bob, his face disguised by a latex mask. But it didn't matter; in wrestling, the ends always justify the means. Randy Orton had beaten another legend.

CASKETS & MORE

Orton's victory restored the luster to his claim of being a legend killer, but it was hardly the end of his showdown with Undertaker. In fact, with Undertaker's *WrestleMania* streak safe and Orton's reputation restored, they started having some real fun . . . and plenty of mayhem.

On the September 9, 2005, *SmackDown!* show, Randy Orton taunted Undertaker by displaying a large (literally) check for his retirement fund. But the joke was on Orton as a bolt of lightning, presumably summoned by the unseen Undertaker, struck the check and set it on fire.

The following week, Randy and his father brought a coffin to the show as Orton and Undertaker prepared to meet in a rematch. The casket turned out to hold a life-sized wax imitation of Undertaker. Whatever voodoo the Ortons were planning failed to spook Undertaker, let alone kill him. Undertaker escaped an RKO and piledrove Randy to the mat for the victory.

The wax figure showed up the next week on *Smack-Down!* as Randy and his dad gave a kind of mock funeral for Undertaker. Randy admitted having lost the previous week's match—but now claimed that he had outpsyched the Dead Man. It was a bold claim, completely obliterated when the wax dummy turned out to be the real Undertaker, who chokeslammed his shocked antagonist into the coffin and then chased him from the arena.

The showdown built to a Casket match at *No Mercy*, the early October Pay-Per-View held in Texas that year. The rules of the match called for Undertaker to put *both* Ortons into the casket to win—a handicap that proved his undoing.

The match began with a chant of "'Taker!" from the crowd as Undertaker squared off against his two opponents. The Ortons took turns getting punched around in the first few minutes, until a low blow by Cowboy Bob felled the Dead Man.

Undertaker absorbed a few dozen shots and falls before he was able to bounce back. Stunning Cowboy Bob with a headbutt, he threw the older man into the casket and went to work on junior.

Randy was ready. His father scrambled out of the coffin and together they pushed Undertaker into it. Undertaker muscled his way out and dominated the action for the next five or six minutes. Going against two men was difficult, and Undertaker found himself vulnerable no matter which way he turned. Pushed up on the ropes in the corner, he fell victim to a kind of double Orton Superplex—a super-suplex off the ropes that sent him between both Ortons.

Had it been a conventional match, Cowboy Bob would have gotten the pin. But the idea was to get Undertaker into the coffin—an idea that failed when Undertaker reversed another attempted Orton double Superplex into a DDT that took both down.

Outside the ring, Undertaker grabbed a steel chair and smacked Randy into the coffin. Cowboy Bob tried to hit Undertaker with a fire extinguisher, but Undertaker turned in time and started pounding him instead. He got the older Orton into a triangle choke on the edge of the ring, then pushed him into the casket as the crowd chanted, "Rest in peace!"

The Ortons were down but not out. Randy managed to pull Undertaker into the box with them. Undertaker punched his way out, following Randy into the ring as Cowboy Bob slumbered on the casket floor, apparently unconscious.

After a seesaw battle in the ring, Undertaker gave Randy Orton a Last Ride Powerbomb that left him stunned. The Dead Man carried the unconscious wrestler to the casket, prepared to dump him in with his dear ol' dad. But when the lid opened, Cowboy Bob emerged with the fire extinguisher, blasting the powder into Undertaker's face.

Cowboy Bob rolled the blinded Undertaker into the coffin. Undertaker managed to pull Randy in with him and the two wrestlers battled below the closed lid. Then the top popped open and Randy grabbed a chair, clocking Undertaker. Seconds later, the two Ortons slammed the lid tight.

It wasn't over.

The Ortons attacked the coffin with an ax, poured gasoline on it, and set it on fire. If the bit reminded the crowd of Undertaker's feud a few years before with Kane, no one mentioned it. In fact, except for a few shrieks, the audience remained silent as the flames shot toward the ceiling, defying the first efforts by the security people to extinguish them.

DEAD NO MORE

Undertaker was dead.

He'd been dead before, but this time it looked like he might really *be* dead. He didn't show up on *SmackDown!* the next week . . . or the week after that. In fact, he didn't show up that month at all. And when the *SmackDown!* Superstars began vying for a place in a showdown with their *Raw* rivals at *Survivor Series*, planned for the end of November, Undertaker was nowhere to be found.

Maybe he really *was* dead.

Or maybe he was waiting for the right time to reappear, like at the climax of *Survivor Series*, just after Randy Orton had led *SmackDown!* to victory. As Randy began to celebrate with the promotion's other wrestlers, Undertaker's bell began to toll.

The Druids carried a coffin in from the back, and Orton looked as if he were seeing a ghost.

A flash of lightning. The coffin caught on fire. There was smoke, flames. Then Undertaker pushed his way out of the upright casket. He cleared the ring, then glared at Orton across the arena, running his thumb across his throat.

ARMAGEDDON

The climax of the story line came at *Armageddon*, December 18, 2005, as Randy Orton and Undertaker fought a Hell in a Cell match.

The opening of the contest saw Orton return to the running style he had tried in their very first get-together. But with his father locked outside the cage, Randy seemed at an immediate disadvantage. Undertaker ruled the beginning of the fight, moving at a slow pace but seemingly able to push it up a notch whenever he cared to. Using his fists, feet, and skull, he punished Randy Orton in as many ways as he could think of over the first five minutes.

Then he pulled a chair out from under the ring and punished him some more.

Orton began to bleed.

A chain found its way into the cage. Undertaker grabbed it from Orton and wrapped it around Orton's neck. He seemed more interested in torturing his opponent than pinning him — then again, Orton had done much to earn his wrath.

Orton finally rallied, catching Undertaker before he could slam a set of stairs on him. Orton grabbed the chain and started choking Undertaker, using his legs for leverage. Undertaker turned around and climbed back into the ring, escaping with the help of a headbutt.

Slightly dazed, Undertaker made his way out to the apron, where he made the mistake of getting too close to the fence. "Cowboy" Bob Orton grabbed him through the links and held him for his son, who took a few pops before Undertaker sent him flying with a counterpunch.

The Dead Man turned on Cowboy Bob, who'd gotten his hand stuck in the fencing. It wasn't Undertaker who did the most damage: As Randy ran at his opponent, the Dead Man ducked away.

Cowboy Bob couldn't.

"Great minds collide," said one of the commentators as father and son fell to the floor.

BLOODIED BUT UNBOWED

Undertaker had been cut somewhere along the way and now blood covered both him and Randy. Orton managed to kick out of several attempted pins, then grabbed the rope to slip out of another. Ducking an Undertaker charge, he caught him in the top rope—a kind of recurring motif in their matches. An Orton low blow—another motif—put Undertaker on the canvas.

Orton had set up a table in the ring earlier but never had a chance to use it. Now he laid Undertaker out on it, climbed on the ropes, and did a Frog Splash onto him, sending him through the table.

Thinking he was in control, Orton put Undertaker on the ropes in the corner and climbed over him to inflict a bit of punishment before the pin. Raising his arms, he beckoned the crowd to recognize his greatness.

Either he waited a bit too long, or his greatness wasn't nearly as profound as he thought. Undertaker responded to the jeers by picking Randy up and carrying him into the middle of the ring.

The ref had been knocked out in the fracas. As the fight continued, a replacement entered the cage and made the mistake of leaving the door open. Cowboy Bob saw his chance and slipped inside, holding an urn — Undertaker's urn, which supposedly gave him control of Undertaker.

That didn't seem to work, so Orton knocked out the replacement ref and tried to go after Undertaker himself. The Dead Man intercepted him. After recovering his urn, Undertaker crowned both Ortons and Tombstoned them into submission, pinning Randy to the cheers of the crowd.

15

MATT HARDY VS. EDGE

Does life imitate art? Or is it the other way around? In wrestling, it can be hard to tell the difference.

FRIENDS & ENEMIES

As one half of their respective tag teams, Matt Hardy and Edge began facing off against each other in 1998. Their high-flying cruiserweight styles won great favor with a sizable segment of fans, who admired their acrobatics and willingness to slam their bodies around the ring.

In the spring of 2002, the Hardy Boys rescued female wrestler Lita just as she was about to be pummeled by Essa Rios. Lita joined them and the trio became known as Team Extreme.

Lita and Matt Hardy were lovers outside the ropes, and after Matt and Lita kissed on *Raw* in February 2001, their relationship became part of the show. Things were never smooth. At one point, it looked like Lita was going to dump

Matt for Eddie Guerrero; at another, Matt's brother Jeff moved in.

Lita was involved in various permutations as a love interest and potential love interest on *Raw* until finally, in 2004, she reunited with Matt. A three-way conflict developed between them and Kane; Lita ended up married to Kane, whom she tormented as the wife from hell (figuratively, despite Kane's own backstory).

REAL LIFE

If the stories were filled with twists and turns, the two lovers' real lives outside the ring were no less complex. At some point in 2005, while still in her relationship with Matt, Lita started seeing Edge. The affair violated the unofficial rules of the wrestling locker room: You don't get involved with another wrestler's boy- or girlfriend. Edge and Hardy were friends in real life, which added to the soap opera nature of the affair.

Around the time that the sleeping arrangements became public knowledge, Matt Hardy left WWE. Fans immediately blamed Edge and Lita. The wrestlers were greeted with derogatory chants whenever they appeared.

Meanwhile, Hardy and WWE worked out a new contract, and within two or three months he was back with the company, just in time to take part in a showdown with Edge and Lita.

SPEAK NOW, OR FOREVER . . .

The story line got going toward the end of May 2005, when Lita announced that she was going to divorce Kane. At the same time, Edge revealed on the show that he and Lita had been having an affair.

A few weeks of animosity between Kane and Edge followed. At the beginning of June, Lita told the audience that she and Edge were thinking of getting married in Las Vegas when they wrestled there at the *Vengeance* Pay-Per-View at the end of the month.

As it turned out, their wedding was held on *Raw* in Phoenix on June 20 and was a blissful affair—or it would have been had Kane not appeared when the minister asked if anyone objected. He objected rather violently, and the two lovers were barely able to escape with their lives. Kane went on to beat Edge the following week at *Vengeance*.

Then Matt Hardy's music brought the crowd to its feet. Hardy didn't appear—Edge and Lita nervously claimed it was their own little gag—but the incident foreshadowed his reappearance on the show a few weeks later.

Hardy showed up for real on July 11. He invaded the dressing area backstage and then interrupted a match between Edge and Kane.

"I'm going to make Edge's life a living hell," he screamed before being dragged from the arena by a team of security people. "Screw WWE!"

The war was on.

IS IT REAL, OR IS IT NOT?

Hardy's rants included denouncements of WWE personnel and seemed very real. Many fans who prided themselves on knowing supposedly backstage information weren't sure if what they were seeing was real or not. The emotions were so raw (excuse the pun) that it was genuinely hard at times to know where the line was.

The story became the perfect blend of reality, sport, and fiction characterizing the best rivalries in wrestling. Reasonable doubt forced viewers to suspend their disbelief as they tuned in week after week.

At the same time, things must have been genuinely difficult for all involved. Yet they somehow managed to continue with it despite, or maybe at times because of, their real emotions.

Hardy's signing with WWE wasn't officially announced until the beginning of August, adding to the speculation. The tension built as Edge and Matt Hardy maneuvered toward a showdown at *SummerSlam* on August 21 in Washington, D.C.

SUMMERSLAM

A roar went up from the crowd as Hardy appeared in the runway at the arena. He was the clear crowd favorite, and the cheering didn't stop as he ran down to the ring. Edge met him on the mat outside the ropes, and the two began fighting immediately.

It was all Hardy, with Edge finally diving into the ring to escape. The bell sounded, and Hardy put Edge onto the canvas, swinging his fists and not caring, or at least not seeming to, about getting a pin.

Edge managed to stop the onslaught with a headbutt. Though dazed, he started delivering haymakers, pummeling Hardy against the ropes. A spear through the ropes took Hardy out to the mat, but Edge ended up there as well.

There weren't many moves in the first five minutes of the match, just general pounding back and forth. Edge, locked in the corner, scooted out from under Hardy, leaving his opponent's face to fall onto the top of the ring post.

Bleeding, Hardy was now an easy target for Edge, who pushed him back into the ring with a flurry of punches. Hardy didn't retreat, urging Edge to keep coming even though the blood was making it hard for him to see. A few kicks to the face, and Hardy was down in the middle of the ring.

Then, with only five minutes gone in the match, the referee stopped it.

STREET FIGHTS AND BRACES

Hardy had busted his head open on the ring post and seemed unable to fight back. But he was back in action the following night on *Raw* against Rob Conway. He lost again, then was assaulted by Edge at the end of the match, keeping their feud alive.

Between the two fights, Hardy looked to the world as if he had sustained a severe concussion, but it didn't stop him from engaging in a hellacious *Raw* street fight August 29 in Tampa. There was more wrestling in this battle, but it ended with sparks flying—literally—as the two wrestlers collapsed into a pile of electrical equipment and the power was cut. When the lights came back, both Hardy and Edge were in neck braces.

Raw GM Eric Bischoff set up a Steel Cage match for the pair at *Unforgiven* in September. In the weeks leading up to it, Lita and Edge continued to hound Hardy, diverting his attention and, in Lita's case, taunting him with sex he couldn't have. Whenever she could get her hands on Hardy, Lita laid a twist of fate on him—her version of a cutter, a move Hardy also used.

IN A CAGE

Like most of the matches between Edge and Hardy, *Unforgiven* began with a straight exchange of blows, more boxing than wrestling. Edge took several early shots at leaving the ring—climbing the cage and then nearly slipping through the door—but Hardy pulled him back.

When Edge finally got the advantage by kicking Hardy into the middle of the ring from the top turnbuckle, his thoughts turned to punishment rather than victory. Vaulting downward, he hit Hardy with a dropkick at the back of the head, spinning him into the canvas.

The next few minutes were Edge's. Grinning widely, he alternated wrestling moves with punches as he punished his opponent. Still, Hardy had the strength to kick out of two attempted pins and even survived a powerbomb against the steel cage.

"Har-dy! Har-dy!" chanted the crowd, firmly on his side.

An Edge powerbomb on Hardy from the top of the corner ropes stunned both wrestlers. Desperate, a few moments later Hardy bit Edge's hand. Edge ran him to the corner, climbed on the ropes, then fell face-first against the post in a move that echoed the one that had taken Hardy out in their first meeting.

The result was far less bloody, but now Hardy had the advantage. He tied Edge in the ropes and gave him a fist-lashing. Screaming like a madman, Hardy circled the prostrate Edge, preferring to punish his enemy rather than leave the cage and win the match. It was Edge's turn to bleed, and he did so profusely, his blood covering the canvas.

Interference from the referee gave Edge the chance to spear Hardy, ending the onslaught.

The two wrestlers made their way to the top rope, then plunged to the canvas, where they lay dazed. Lita ran in and hit Hardy but got a little more than she bargained for—a twist of fate that left her temporarily unconscious.

Hardy climbed to the top of the cage. With no one in his way, he could have easily descended to the floor and won. But that wasn't what the match was about for him. Jumping from the top of the cage, he landed on Edge's face. Seconds later, the ref counted out his unconscious opponent.

UP IN THE AIR

The next night on *Raw*, Edge complained that it was impossible for both of them to stay in the company. GM Eric Bischoff agreed and set up the final confrontation, a Ladder match at *Raw*'s WWE Homecoming show October 3 in Dallas.

Hardy and Edge had been involved in some wild Ladder action during their days as tag team opponents, and so it was fitting that the conflict climaxed with a Ladder bout. The Money-in-the-Bank format called for the winner to grab a briefcase hanging above the ring. Inside was a contract allowing him to stay at *Raw*; the loser was *SmackDown!* bound.

The action started with a cheap shot by Edge as Hardy emerged from backstage. Hardy recovered in time to catch him on the ladder and a seesaw fight ensued.

Once again, the ladder's use as a weapon was limited only by the imagination of the wrestlers. Hardy put the ladder upside down, inserted Edge in it, then climbed up the sides before using it to squeeze his opponent.

In case there was any doubt, the crowd reaffirmed its allegiance with a Hardy chant soon after the bout began. Edge clearly had the upper hand over the first five or six minutes, with Hardy chasing him up the ladder and just barely keeping him from grabbing the briefcase. He threw Edge off, into a second ladder, then fell himself as Edge's rebound toppled his own perch.

Outside the ring, Hardy set up a ladder and dove into the crowd, laying a cross-body on Edge to knock him out. His advantage was short-lived, as Lita jumped on his back. Edge recovered and clocked him with a kendo stick below the belt; the low blow took away more than just breath.

There were now two ladders set up side by side in the ring. As Edge climbed toward the briefcase, Hardy came after him. A twist of fate off the ladder took Edge to the floor outside the ring. Hardy couldn't recover quickly enough. With his hands on the briefcase, he was swatted down by Lita and the kendo stick. She took the ladder out from under him, leaving him dangling by the briefcase.

Edge jumped in and, using Hardy as a swing, pulled him down into the ropes. Edge and Lita tied him into the top ropes, Lita locking her limbs around his arms to keep him there.

TRUE LIFE AND MORE

The match ended the trio's showdown. Matt Hardy went to *SmackDown!*, where he began tangling with several Superstars. Edge, after recovering from an injury, moved into his Rated-R Superstar phase.

Fans may have loved the showdown because it made them feel like insiders, privy to the wrestlers' real lives. But the true achievement was the wrestlers' ability to turn those lives—and deep emotions—into entertainment. The physical strain in the ring storytelling was matched by the real-life strain of simply telling the story, making the showdown a unique achievement.

16

REY MYSTERIO VS. EDDIE GUERRERO

The 2005 saga between Rey Mysterio and Eddie Guerrero was a clash not just of Mexican wrestlers, but of friends. Coming just before Guerrero's tragic death that November, the showdown gave two of the most athletic wrestlers in the trade a chance to work their magic before millions of fans.

LUCHA LIBRE

Both men came from families with rich ties to Mexican wrestling. While the general rules of wrestling are the same in Mexico as they are in the United States, aficionados find the brand of wrestling practiced south of the Rio Grande to be a bit freer and perhaps faster than that in the north. Called *lucha libre*, the Mexican style makes great use of leaps and flying moves, placing a premium on a wrestler's athleticism rather than sheer size or strength.

It's not quite fair to U.S. wrestlers to say that *luchadores* are quicker or more agile, but as a general rule a successful Mexican wrestler seems at least part acrobat when he dominates the ring. That's one reason that Mexican audiences seem to prefer wrestlers in what Americans consider the cruiserweight division, rather than heavyweight. (Cruiserweight is usually defined as under 220 pounds. Mexican wrestling uses a different weight system from the United States, so the analogy is not precise.)

The most obvious difference in style from one side of the border to the other is the use of the mask in Mexican wrestling. In fact, many observers point out that the mask has almost religious significance in the Mexican version of the sport.

With their connection to the ancient Aztecs, the masks — or *máscaras*—have historical and cultural significance that extends well beyond wrestling. At one time, the masks contained direct references to different native gods, whose attributes or favor the wrestler invoked. Now they tend to be somewhat stylized, chosen more for color and flash.

The importance of the mask in the Mexican tradition can be seen not only in the custom of always wearing the mask in the ring but also in the fact that to take off one's mask is considered a literal losing of face. Doing so in the ring causes immediate disqualification—and implied humiliation. Many wrestlers wear them outside the ring and would not think of doing a public appearance related to wrestling without them. Some of the most emotional matches in Mexico demand that the loser take off his mask, revealing his real face and name.

WWE follows American traditions, and most Mexican wrestlers in the promotion follow the old adage of "When in

Rome . . ." But Rey Mysterio is unique because he always wears the mask. It is part of his personality, an important facet of one of the age's most athletic and successful professional wrestlers.

LIE! CHEAT! STEAL!

Eddie Guerrero's approach was different. He was an underhanded wrestler who could and would do anything to win.

Or as his unofficial slogans put it: "I lie! I cheat! I steal!" and "Cheat to win!"

CHAMPIONS TOGETHER

Mysterio and Guerrero teamed up together in 2005. Working as a tag team at No Way Out in February, they defeated the Basham Brothers to capture the WWE Tag Team Championship. The next few weeks saw them defend their title with ease, as no other team could match the pair's combination of speed, strength, and agility.

Chavo Guerrero spent the month sowing dissension between the pair, telling Eddie that Rey was holding him back, and telling Rey that Eddie couldn't be trusted. In mid-March, with neither set for a WrestleMania solo match, Eddie suggested they wrestle each other. And so they did.

While still partners — there was friction but no break — the wrestlers went at each other with great abandon. Mysterio literally flew into the match from the top rope; Guerrero tried to finish his friend with his famous Frog Splash, his signature close. In the end, Mysterio managed to come out on top.

The two combatants shook hands at the end of the match. But their partnership had begun to crack.

The frustration was on full display on the April 21 *Smack-Down!* when Mysterio and Guerrero defended their championship against MNM (Joey Mercury and Johnny Nitro, managed by Melina Perez).

Mercury and Nitro were new to WWE; they'd just come up from Ohio Valley, a regional wrestling and development company where many WWE stars have gotten their start. To say that the veteran team of Mysterio and Guerrero was heavily favored would be to understate the situation by half. But behind the scenes, Guerrero and Mysterio were having problems getting along.

When Guerrero and Mysterio lost, the result shocked everyone, including Guerrero, who blamed it on his partner and took out his frustrations by slamming him to the mat after the winners were declared.

A rematch was set for the following *SmackDown!* Once again, Guerrero and Mysterio were heavily favored. Just before the match, the two seemed to have patched things up. In the locker room, Guerrero delivered an impassioned speech about how close he felt to Mysterio, even saying he cared for him like a brother.

Things soured out in the ring. Mysterio accidentally hit Guerrero; Guerrero thought it was done on purpose. He was ready to strand Mysterio, leaving him to face the two wrestlers alone. Only the pleas from the crowd—a rowdy bunch in the working-class town of Birmingham, England—brought Guerrero back to the ring. But once there, he did little more than watch MNM trash Mysterio.

Match decided, Guerrero walked from the arena as his erstwhile partner continued to be pummeled. It was a brutal betrayal, marked by the crowd with a chanted "Eddie sucks."

The lines were drawn. With two of *SmackDown!*'s most bankable stars feuding, the entire franchise was drawn into the conflict. Wrestlers took sides as the heat built, literally and figuratively, through the summer. Mysterio dominated most of the confrontations, winning at *Judgment Day*, the *Great American Bash*, and *SummerSlam*.

A FAMILY THING

Their meeting at *SummerSlam* that August was probably the most talked about confrontation in the series. It featured a Ladder match that became a classic of its kind. As was to be expected, the wrestling was superb, a highly athletic match between two pros at the top of their careers.

But that wasn't all that made it interesting.

On the June 30 *SmackDown!* Guerrero threatened to reveal a secret about Mysterio and his son Dominick. He clearly relished his secret and the power it gave him—even as Mysterio trashed him in the ring.

Both men's families pleaded with Guerrero not to reveal what he knew. When Mysterio and Guerrero met at the *Great American Bash* in July, at stake was Guerrero's promise not to reveal the secret; if Guerrero lost, he said, he'd keep his mouth shut.

But Guerrero wasn't about to keep the secret even though he did lose. In true turncoat fashion, he revealed all the following week: He, Eddie Guerrero, was the "real" father of Rey's adopted eight-year-old son, Dominick.

The details his parentage were revealed over the following weeks as installments in "Eddie's Bedtime Stories." He claimed that he had had a child out of wedlock (Dominick) while his own marriage was going through hard times. He said he allowed Mysterio and his wife to adopt the child as their own when they couldn't conceive; they had kept it a secret from their son and everyone else. Now Guerrero wanted the boy back.

The *SummerSlam 2005* match that August had all of that emotion simmering in the background: bad blood between former friends, each of whom felt betrayed; personal animosity and jealousy over family relations; a feeling of deep resentment over the disruption of personal lives. At stake in the outcome of the fight was custody of Dominick.

LADDER MATCH

A Ladder match is decided when one wrestler successfully retrieves an object—usually a championship belt—from the top rung of a ladder in the ring. In this case, Dominick's custody papers were hanging from a rafter in an attaché case reachable only by the ladder.

After a start that featured a series of Guerrero cheap shots, the two wrestlers began flying around the ring, sometimes under their own power, sometimes not. Though 0–6 against Mysterio to that point, Guerrero succeeded in getting the upper hand, attacking his opponent while they were both outside the ring and using the ladder as a weapon.

A Mysterio dropkick off the top rope knocked Guerrero from the ladder. But early injuries in the match hamstrung Mysterio. The two wrestlers resorted to boxing each other on the ladder as they both tried to reach the briefcase. Guerrero regained command and pressed his attack, using the ladder effectively to batter his opponent.

Now fully in control, Guerrero decided to rub in his victory. He took the ladder and placed it over the fallen Mysterio, who was lying on his back near the center of the ring. Taunting Mysterio, Guerrero climbed up and reached for the briefcase — only to have Mysterio rally and pull the ladder out from under him.

A vicious series followed, with Guerrero slamming Mysterio to the mat several times before giving him a vertical suplex that sent Mysterio onto the prone ladder.

Once more on the ladder, Guerrero was interrupted when his wife, Vickie, ran into the ring and pleaded with him not to break up the Mysterio family. When her husband refused to back down, she took matters into her own hands, pushing him from the ladder.

As husband and wife continued to struggle, Mysterio got up off the canvas, climbed the ladder, and retrieved the papers. Dominick remained his.

The crowd leaped to its feet.

END OF THE LINE

The final contest in the feud was a Steel Cage match in early September. Guerrero declared before the match that he had nothing left to lose, and he fought that way, his usual sunny personality displaced by a brooding but lethal presence. The fight had a solemn tone, starting with an exchange of punches that led to a monkeyflip and a powerbomb flurry as the grapplers traded moves.

With Guerrero and Mysterio fighting it out at the top of the cage, both men were injured falling to the canvas. Guerrero managed to crawl from the cage, which would have given him the victory, but he decided to return and pin the injured Mysterio instead, gaining a more satisfying win and putting a stop to the feud.

Two months later, Guerrero would die of heart problems. Mysterio has spoken passionately of their friendship and dedicated his championship at *WrestleMania 22* the following year to Guerrero. Among his many tributes to the man who brought out some of his best performances, he adopted Guerrero's signature Frog Splash as his own.

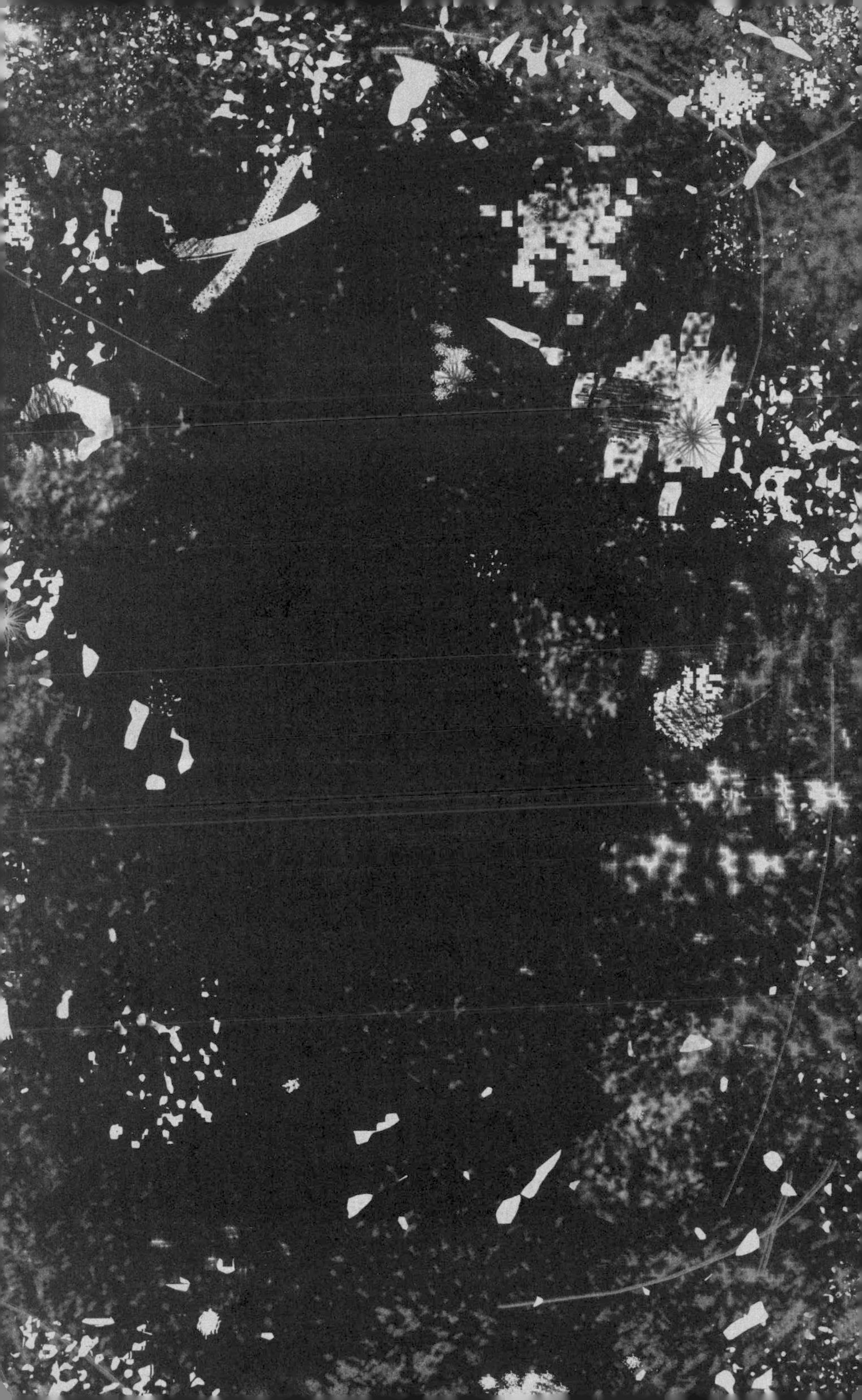

17

BATISTA
VS. TRIPLE H

There comes a time when the student is no longer the apprentice; when, in fact, he has become the master. It is a difficult time for both him and his teacher—a dangerous time. Woe onto the mentor who holds his student down when he is ready to soar on his own. For then the master will have a war on his hands—as Triple H discovered when the Animal was ready to fly.

EVOLUTION

Batista joined WWE in 2003 and proved himself an adept student, learning the nuances of the ring from two of the best wrestlers around, Triple H and Ric Flair. As a member of Triple H's heel stable, Evolution, he began as an enforcer, doing Triple H's bidding. Soon, his look and plain-talk style struck a note with the crowd. The cheers grew louder and louder when he stepped into the ring. Gradually, his skills improved, and he began to feel his oats—and realized he was meant to be more than just a sidekick.

EVOLUTION DISSOLUTION

The break came in January 2005 when Triple H, then the World Heavyweight Champ, realized Batista had a legitimate shot at the title. A win at *Royal Rumble* gave Batista the right to challenge one WWE champion, and it soon became clear to Triple H that his onetime sidekick had bigger ambitions than carrying his suitcase.

Triple H told Batista that he didn't mind the challenge and even predicted they would be going against each other at *WrestleMania*. But he was secretly worried. The year before, Triple H had torpedoed fellow Evolution member Randy Orton for similar reasons; now he set out to do the same to Batista.

JBL had been harassing Evolution, and Triple H set out to use JBL's animosity as a way to take Batista out of the picture. He wanted Batista to focus on JBL, jumping to *SmackDown!* and going after his title (WWE Championship) rather than Triple H's. But he was too clever to say that.

Triple H saved Batista after JBL's limo nearly ran him over. Batista then showed up on *SmackDown!*—where JBL was starring—but rather than confronting him, he smashed his limo to pieces. JBL, meanwhile, claimed he knew nothing of the attempted hit-and-run.

On February 20, Batista showed up at the tail end of the *SmackDown!* Pay-Per-View *No Way Out*, trashing JBL's cabinet. With speculation growing that Batista would jump to *SmackDown!* for a shot at JBL, Triple H confessed to Flair that he had actually arranged the limo swipe at Batista.

Unfortunately for Triple H, Batista heard his confession. He left Evolution but stayed on *Raw*, aiming for Triple H's title.

WRESTLEMANIA 21

"I'm the game," sang Mötorhead as Triple H was announced at *WrestleMania 21*.

Water spraying from his mouth, Triple H snarled his way into the ring, ready to start. A few minutes later, Batista entered. He didn't have a live band behind him, but he was looking just as ferocious.

The two wrestlers exchanged a long glare in the middle of the ring. Triple H made a threat. Batista thought it was funny and started to laugh.

Neither man was laughing a short time later. They went toe to toe, sizing up each other's strength. The match was billed as a fight between strength (Batista) and skill (Triple H), but the difference was only a matter of degree; neither wrestler truly lacked the other quality.

Flicked away after an early tangle, Triple H suddenly looked as if he realized he faced a fight. Batista took over, powering out of a Pedigree and slamming Triple H to the mat. For the next several minutes, it was all Batista.

Then Triple H showed why he was champion.

Sending Batista from the ring, he took advantage of a diversion by Evolution stablemate Ric Flair to sneak up on him and slam him into the steps. A few minutes later, Flair managed to choke Batista while he lay beneath the ropes. Triple H pummeled him with his elbow, dropping again and again, until finally the crowd began to implore Batista to fight back.

Revived by the chants, Batista struggled to change the tide. Surviving a number of backbreakers and similar attacks, the Animal nonetheless had trouble finding his way until he connected with a series of fists and backed Triple H across the ring.

The middle of the match was relatively even, though Batista didn't get a chance to try a pin until roughly fifteen minutes had passed. Now it was a slow war of attrition, both big men trading power blows inside and outside the ring.

A catapult against the ring post dazed Triple H and bloodied his forehead. Batista began punishing him, sending his erstwhile mentor against the steps before dragging him to the center of the ring. The crowd counted out the blows.

Somehow, Triple H kicked out of the pin attempt that followed. Escaping from the ring, he took advantage of more interference from Flair to grab a chair and try a sneak attack. The ref caught him, and then so did Batista, who hurled him back into the ring, weaponless.

Flair jumped in, trying to smack him with the championship belt, but Batista slammed him to the canvas.

Diverted, Batista was an easy target. Triple H clocked him with the championship belt and dove down, hoping to make the fall stick. Batista kicked out in the nick of time, bringing the crowd to its feet.

A spinebuster, and then the Animal began pounding his chest.

Do you want to see the end?

A low blow postponed the pin, but only for seconds. Batista used his strength to block a desperate attempt at a Pedigree, then reversed it into a backward slam.

The Animal turned to the crowd. Arms outstretched, he held his thumbs up, gladiator style, then turned them down.

They loved it.

A Batista bomb obliterated Triple H, and the roof came off the auditorium.

"GAME OVER"

There was far too much bad blood between the two wrestlers for the story to end there.

The next major match between Triple H and Batista came at *Backlash*, May 1. They traded antagonisms right up to the match. Triple H, never one to take a loss easily, tried hammering Batista with a sledgchammer in the shows after the match, only to see Batista split it into splinters and proclaim, "Game over!"

The two wrestlers got to pick their enemy's opponent in a series of Pick Your Poison matchups, though of course neither could completely get over the other. Triple H claimed that Batista had gotten "lucky" at *WrestleMania*, and that luck would be reversed at *Backlash*.

"Your eyes told me the one thing you feared—it is the Pedigree!" hc howled.

The Animal said he intended on being champ for quitc a while to come.

BACKLASH

Sporting new blue trunks and shooting off a full run of pyro, Batista took to the ring as champ at the May 1 Pay-Per-View. But it was Triple H who seemed the different man at the contest, starting out more ferocious, maybe more desperate, than he had at *WrestleMania*. He quickly took the momentum. But after several attempts to set up the Pedigree failed, he found himself flying over the ropes.

It didn't take long for him to get back on offense. When Batista came out to challenge him, Triple H grabbed him and began flipping him back and forth over the barrier that kept the crowd back. Triple H couldn't afford for the match

to end there—a disqualification would keep the championship belt on Batista—and so he finally hauled his opponent
back inside the ropes.

Flair—demonstrating why he was billed as the "dirtiest
player in the business"—once again looked for a chance to
interfere. He found it when Batista rolled out below the
ropes, pummeling the big man against the side of the ring.

Batista showed little sign of wear as he kicked out of three
attempted pins in machine-gun succession. Now the worm
began to turn. Rallying his strength, Batista once again threw
Triple H from the ring, then pursued him around the apron
area, flinging him into anything and everything handy.

Back in the ring, Batista slammed Triple H to the canvas,
then grabbed the ropes and began shaking them like an animal gone berserk. Flair managed to sneak the championship
belt into the ring, and while the ref's back was turned, Triple
H clocked Batista in the head with it.

Triple H thought he got a slow count as Batista escaped
the pin, and for a moment it looked as if he was going to
strangle the referee. But it was Batista the ref had to worry
about. Charging across the ring, he missed Triple H but sent
the official spinning to the floor.

Triple H finally landed a Pedigree, rolling onto his opponent for a pin. The ref was still out of the ring and couldn't
count the fall. Flair picked him up and pushed him in, where
he lay, dreaming of matches from days gone by.

Neither Triple H nor Flair could revive him, and by the
time another ref appeared from the back, Batista had risen to
his feet. He survived a facebuster, then unleashed a series of
clotheslines on Triple H, who found himself barely able to
stand in the corner.

Trying to get at his adversary, Triple H kicked the replacement ref in the groin, sending him down—the second zebra on the mat.

A vicious low blow by Triple H failed to slow the champ, as he managed a Batista bomb and held on while the still-dazed ref counted out the pin.

HELL IN A CELL

Having lost twice, Triple H was no longer in a direct line for a shot at the championship. Instead, a group of *Raw* wrestlers began competing in a Gold Rush tournament for a chance to grab Batista's title. Ultimately, Edge won the tourney—only to be downed by Batista on May 23 on *Raw*.

At the end of the match, Triple H came out and challenged Batista to a Hell in a Cell showdown. With help from Ric Flair, whom Batista had saved from a beatdown the week before, Triple H Pedigreed the champ to his keister. The two men prepared for a showdown at *Vengeance*.

The match was their third headline Pay-Per-View, but the cell put a different spin on the proceedings. They began brawling even before they got to their event, fighting it out backstage after Triple H interrupted a promo Batista was taping.

"The devil's duplex!" quipped J.R. as Triple H entered the ring, and it was, with both wrestlers trying early on to use the fenced-in walls as a weapon.

Batista had the initial advantage, tossing Triple H against the walls again and again. Triple H returned the favor, using the ring post as his target.

Triple H realized he couldn't win if he used only the walls or ring. Reaching beneath the mat, he found a chain and worked it into a multipronged whip, tormenting his opponent. Then he used it to hang Batista by the neck off the ropes.

He still couldn't get a submission.

Batista finally took the chain and used it as a whip, taking a lap around the ring at Triple H's expense. By the time Triple H got back into the ring, his forehead was covered with blood.

He gained time with a spinebuster that seemed to come out of nowhere. Rolling out of the ring, Triple H reached below the ring and pulled out a chair . . . wrapped in barbed wire.

WIRED FOR PAIN

A hard shot to Batista's back put him down and got his blood flowing—mostly on the canvas.

"Holy shit!" chanted the crowd.

Batista took another hard shot before desperation drove him to deck Triple H with a blow to the chest. A clothesline leveled the challenger—and then Batista picked up the barbed-wire chair.

Triple H took a shot in the face and rolled down, his whole body jerking in pain. When he stopped rolling, Batista took the chair and used it like a cheese grater on Triple H's head.

Batista had overwhelming crowd support, and the fans chanted for much of the match.

Triple H tried to slam Batista into the chair with a Pedigree but was too weak. Reversing out of the hold, Batista danced around, then did a Powerslam that sent Triple H onto the barbs.

Punctured but not pulverized, Triple H recovered. A

DDT sent Batista's face into the chair a few moments later. Back and forth the two wrestlers fought, until finally, outside the ring, Triple H reached below the curtain and found a sledgehammer.

Batista kicked it from his hands, then initiated a slugging match that lasted a full minute or more. Seemingly in control, the champion set up for a Batista bomb—only to have Triple H break out of it, flipping him into a back-body drop.

Sending the sledgehammer against Batista's skull, Triple H took another shot at a pin but couldn't get the count.

Chain and hammer flying, the two men attacked each other without mercy or hope of redemption. Triple H climbed the turnbuckle and dove toward his enemy with his chain-wrapped fist—only to be repelled by the sledgehammer, which caught him in the throat.

Batista began punching Triple H, trying to lay him down for the fall. Failing that, he sent Triple H over the ropes, then chased him outside, tossing him into the stairs.

"That sickening thud was a human body striking steel!" moaned J.R.

Back in the ring again, Triple H summoned his courage and adrenaline for one last, desperate attempt. Suddenly, things seemed to fall into place. He got Batista into a textbook Pedigree and . . .

Batista rolled over and kicked out.

Triple H still had the advantage. Dragging his enemy to the base of the steel stairs—Batista had carried it into the ring earlier—he prepared to drive his opponent's skull into the metal. Batista countered, smacking Triple H into the base with a spinebuster.

Hoisted toward the rafters for a Batista bomb, Triple H

grabbed the sledgehammer and swung. His blow missed, and after he was slammed to the canvas the crowd counted him down. The ref was just there for validation.

BATISTA'S GREATEST

The two wrestlers had gone through a war. There was nothing else for them to prove against each other. Batista moved on to a feud with JBL; he would get injured in January and have to relinquish his title. He would have many other memorable matches, but he would call his series with Triple H the greatest of his career, lauding Triple H's exploits and abilities in his memoir, *Batista Unleashed*.

18

EDGE
VS. CENA

Some Superstars have to lie, cheat, and steal to get ahead.

They also have to have a knack for being in the right place at the right time.

Or the wrong place at the wrong time, if you're their opponent. Just ask John Cena, who had his pocket picked by Edge at *New Year's Revolution* in 2006.

Unfortunately for Cena, it was his championship belt that he lost. And while he got it back a few weeks later, he couldn't seem to shake Edge, who returned later in the year to torment him.

REVOLUTION

Cena survived a hellacious Elimination Chamber match at *Revolution* in early January, outlasting Kurt Angle, Carlito, Chris Masters, Shawn Michaels, and Kane to hold on to the championship title he'd won from JBL roughly nine months before.

Battered and exhausted, he knelt in the middle of the ring, blood covering his face, championship belt at his side, gathering himself after victory was declared. Before he could get to his feet, Mr. McMahon came out and announced that Edge was cashing in his Money-in-the-Bank privilege, allowing him to wrestle Cena for the championship.

Edge had won the privilege back at *WrestleMania* the year before; it entitled him to demand a championship match whenever, wherever he wanted. Anyone who didn't realize he'd wait until the best possible moment (for him) didn't know Edge very well.

Cena staggered across the ring, barely able to provide a target for Edge's fists. He kicked out of three pins, but a hard spear smashed him to the canvas for the count.

Perhaps remembering his long career, the crowd got to its feet and cheered Edge's championship, despite the underhanded way he'd won it.

It wasn't true love, though, and it wouldn't last.

EDGE & LITA

Edge's rivalry with Cena intersected with another story involving the Rated-R Superstar. He and Lita were still an item, and he proclaimed that in honor of his winning the championship, they would have sex in the middle of the ring.

They did—or almost did—at the January 9 *Raw*. At a strategic moment, Ric Flair interrupted them. He got a body-slam for his troubles.

That was nothing compared to what Lita got from Cena, who did his own run-in while Edge was dealing with Flair. Cena did an F-U on the scantily clad Lita, ensuring that he and Edge would continue to tangle.

First, though, Edge had to deal with Flair, which he did the next week. Only a last-second run-in by Cena saved Flair from a one-man conchairto and probable maiming.

Their animosity peaked at *Royal Rumble*, January 29, 2006, in Miami.

RUMBLE

Cena entered on a metal scaffold lowered from the ceiling. Some thought it looked like a spaceship; Cena used it like a big diving board, allowing him to jump into the middle of the ring without using the ramp.

Thrown outside the ring, Edge scrambled around, grabbing Lita and tossing her at Cena as a diversion. He followed up with a spear that took Cena against the ring steps. A chant of "Ce-na! Ce-na!" brought Cena back to the ropes, but Edge skidded feet-first across the ring, knocking him back across the barrier and away from the apron area.

Cena got back in just before the referee could count him out. He made it only as far as the ropes, where Edge proceeded to kick and jump on him for more than a minute.

In control, Edge toyed with Cena and the ref, throwing his opponent outside the ropes, rolling back in to break the disqualification count, then going outside to torment Cena some more. But after Edge brought Cena back in for the pin and failed twice to get the fall, the tide began to turn.

Cena caught Edge in midair and set him up for the F-U. Edge poked him in his eyes, forcing a release. Edge managed a foot kick to Cena's face, knocking him down. Edge couldn't cover—and as a matter of fact, didn't try. Instead, he climbed the turnbuckle and with a gleam in his eye leaped at Cena, hitting him with high cross-body that took him to the canvas.

Again, he couldn't get the pin.

A scissors hold, bodychoke—Edge just couldn't find the solution. Cena managed to climb to his feet with Edge on his back. Ducking a spear, Cena got a DDT on Edge as both wrestlers went down.

A flying headbutt by Cena took the starch out of his opponent. Lita distracted the referee just long enough to cost Cena the pin. Cena jumped to his feet, grabbed Lita by the hair, and held her in place as Edge ran toward him. Cena ducked away at the last minute, causing Edge to spear his girlfriend. An F-U, an STFU (a stepover sleeper adapted by Cena), and Edge tapped out for the loss, giving the title back to Cena.

A THREE-WAY

Edge tried to win a rematch two weeks later on a Thursday night *Raw* with Mick Foley as ref. After failing to butter Foley up, Edge lost, a decision he blamed on Foley, with whom he began fighting in the weeks that followed.

Cena and Edge put their rivalry largely on hold until midsummer, when they found themselves in a three-way conflict with Rob Van Dam for the championship belt.

This phase of the conflict began after Van Dam won the WWE Championship belt from Cena under "extreme rules"—he'd been drafted from *Raw* to ECW—at *One Night Stand*, the June 11 Pay-Per-View featuring ECW-brand wrestlers. Edge, partly disguised by a motorcycle helmet, helped set up the win by weakening Cena with a smash through a table before Van Dam got the pin and the title.

Van Dam was also awarded the (revived) ECW championship belt on the new ECW TV show, making him the first wrestler ever to hold both championships at the same time.

The interference and low blows angered Cena, and he vowed to use the same tactics himself—a promise he kept over the next few shows, interfering in ECW matches and generally harassing Van Dam. But he had to wait until *Raw* on June 26 for another title shot.

As the TV match wound down, it looked as if Cena was going to get the pin. Then Edge came in and attacked both men; the disqualification kept the championship belt on Van Dam. Lest anyone think he was playing favorites, Edge also showed up the next night on the ECW show, where once again he speared Van Dam.

The three men faced off July 3 on *Raw*. Van Dam and Cena teamed up at first, beating Edge to a pulp before he could even get out of the corner. The only breaks in the action came as they asked each other to stand back and let the other get his punches in. Finally, they tossed Edge out of the ring and got down to business themselves.

After a short breather, and maybe a kiss from Lita, Edge rebounded. He got back in and exchanged acrobatics with Van Dam. After a flying leap by Van Dam broke up a suplex by Cena on Edge, all three wrestlers lay on the canvas. They got up, took a few shots at each other, then settled into a kind of round-robin slugfest, one punching a second man, who punched the third.

Finally, Edge managed to throw Van Dam from the ring. That only gave Cena the advantage, as he began a furious attack on Edge, eventually tossing him over the ropes.

Lita, still in Edge's corner, tried to even things up by hitting Cena with a steel chair. Cena intercepted her and knocked her out with an F-U. Van Dam was able to take advantage of the interruption, launching his own chair-assisted attack. Cena avoided a five-star Frog Splash from Van Dam, then prepared to pin the champion . . . and would have, had Edge not managed to grab the championship belt and knock Cena away with it. He slid in and got the pin on Van Dam, taking the WWE Championship.

DISQUALIFICATIONS & THEN SOME

Edge and Cena continued the feud alone, with some help from Lita. Cena attacked Edge in his hotel room the following week; a week later Edge and Lita helped Umaga down Cena.

At the July 15 *Saturday Night's Main Event,* a television special aired in prime time, Cena seemed to have won the match and the title when Lita interfered, hauling referee Mike Chioda out of the ring and attacking him. The interference wasn't the product of a blind rage but a clever tactic to end the match by disqualification—thus keeping the title on Edge.

If tempers weren't running hot enough, Edge ensured more animosity by visiting Cena's parents' home in mid-August—and, as he put it, "bitch slapping" Cena's father.

Of course, this was all caught on the camera he had follow them.

The following week, Edge and Cena met to settle things at *SummerSlam*, August 20.

"I keep coming back," said Edge, recounting his long history as champ before the match got under way. "This story is going to have a happy ending . . . in my favor."

The match had an unusual stipulation: If Edge was disqualified, he would lose the title. So he warned Lita not to interfere.

Cena got a rousing ovation from his hometown crowd as he came into the Boston ring. It was all Cena at the top of the match, as his anger over the trashing his father received powered a flurry of punches and knockdowns. Not until Cena charged his way out of the ring did the match regain some equilibrium. Having to be careful because of the DQ rule—an illegal hold would lose it for him after a five count—Edge couldn't get too much traction.

Neither could Cena. After Edge failed several times to get a pin, Cena seemed poised to take back the momentum, but couldn't. A flying Clothesline by Edge—one of the most athletic moves in the series—failed to lead to a pin.

The crowd began chanting, "Let's go Cena!" For maybe the first time in the showdown there seemed to be no dissenters in the arena. The fans were *truly* behind him.

Cena rose from his knees to escape a chin lock. Both men now spent considerable time on the canvas, until Lita distracted Edge by throwing in a chair.

Edge angrily threw it back, and then was slammed by Cena. With Edge down, Cena shook his hand in his face, yelling, "You can't see me!" then went for the pin.

Edge escaped.

Cena was able to hoist Edge up for a slam but couldn't complete it. Both men ran desperately. When they were caught, they barely broke each other's pin attempts. Edge pushed Lita away when she tried to interfere, once more protecting his title.

During one exchange, Lita managed to slip him a pair of brass knuckles unseen by the referee. Then she jumped into the ring and onto Edge's back—he was on Cena's back at the time—and while the ref tossed her from the ring, Edge clocked Cena with the knuckles. He pushed the unconscious Cena over and got the pin.

TLC

The pair had unfinished business, and Cena aimed to settle it at *Unforgiven.* Held September 17 in Toronto, they were in Edge's hometown and fighting in a match believed to benefit Edge, a TLC contest—tables, ladders, and chairs. Once more they were fighting for the title—Edge had unveiled a new design for the championship belt, which he called an R-rated version (an R replaced the center spinner). If Cena lost, he would have to leave *Raw.*

Edge dominated the first few minutes of the contest, bringing in two chairs and two ladders without much interference from Cena. After Cena managed to throw Edge onto one of the ladders he'd set up against the corner ropes, things got more interesting.

Edge powerslammed Cena through the table, provoking a "Cena sucks!" chant from the Edge partisans in the crowd. A few minutes later, Cena was the aggressor, sandwiching Edge in a ladder and using it to guillotine him nearly in half. Screaming, Cena then tried to F-U Edge between the ladder's legs. The pain was so intense Edge tried to tap out, apparently forgetting that tap outs were ignored under the rules of the match.

Cena spent the next few minutes pummeling Edge, to the occasional boos from the crowd.

Staggering, Edge managed to get back in the contest with a chair shot to Cena's head. A spear from one ladder to another put Cena down, coughing on the canvas. Cena was able to catch Edge as he dove down from the twelve-foot ladder. The wrestlers turned their attention from the championship belt to each other, trading smashes outside the ring.

Cena finally got the better of Edge. Leaving him huddled on the apron, he climbed up the ladder. Just as he had his hands on the championship belt, Lita ran in and tipped him over, sending him crashing into a table beyond the rope.

Edge got back in and climbed upward, eyes on the prize. A smash by Lita on Cena sent him tumbling into the ladder, throwing Edge through another table outside. Now alone in the ring, Cena arranged the ladder and tables for one last spot while Edge got to his feet and raced back to the ladder.

Cena climbed up the other side. The pair met in the middle, where Cena put Edge over his shoulders, then dropped him through the two tables near the center of the ring. Cena reached up. He finally had beaten Edge for the championship.

CODA

The next night at *Raw* in Montreal, Edge once more had the Canadian crowd behind him—until he put Cena over by dissing the Montrealers, riffing on the English-French divide in the Quebec province by saying they weren't really Canadians. Later in the show, Cena pounded Edge in a Three-Man Tag match (though Edge won by DQ). The pair, with Lita strategically interfering, continued to meet over the next few weeks. Cena took a Cage match in Topeka; the following week, he and Cena tussled during a women's wrestling match (which Lita won) and a promo before Lita and Cena went at it in a Handicap match where Cena had one hand tied behind his back.

The Handicap opened the way for an ambush by *Smack-Down!* stars, which ended up damaging Cena's left arm.

He won the match anyway.

IN CAGE

The final contest of the series came at a *Raw* show at the beginning of October, as Cena and Edge went at it in a cage.

By now, the wrestlers knew each other very well, and so did the fans. Their allegiances had realigned: Edge was booed loudly during his introduction; Cena, his arm taped, won steady applause. Edge's bad-boy tactics had finally caught up to him.

He wasn't going gently. Edge hammered on the arm, punching, kicking, scratching, trying anything he could to increase Cena's pain. His attack was so ferocious, he almost escaped the cage after only two minutes had gone.

Too bad *almost* doesn't count in wrestling.

Cena pulled him back in and, with the crowd roaring, began giving his opponent an old-fashioned beatdown. Edge kept slipping out of pins. Finally, as Cena climbed the cage to win the contest, Edge grabbed his injured arm and pulled him back. He speared him, taking temporary control of the match.

"*Ce-na! Ce-na!*" implored the crowd.

Cena climbed after Edge, pulling him face-first to the canvas from the top rope. A minute or so later, they were both on the top of the cage, trading blows, each trying to topple the other off. Down to the canvas, against the cage, Cena got a surge of adrenaline and shuffled his way over to fist Edge. Using the cage to avoid an F-U, Edge made a dash for the corner, trying to climb away. Cena caught him but barely escaped a pin as Edge reversed a move.

A desperate leap by Cena stopped Edge as he crawled through the door. Lita, relatively quiet during the match, sprang to life and tried to pull Edge out.

Somewhere along the way, a chair had been thrown into the ring. Cena used it to stop Edge, putting him flush on the canvas. The referee had been knocked out. A second ref tried to get in to count Edge down, but he was run over by Lance Cade and Trevor Murdoch, Edge's allies, who high-lowed Cena and pulled Edge toward the door, hoping to steal the win.

The crowd, sensing what would happen next, began chanting for DX. (DX had faced Cade and Murdoch the week before in a Gauntlet match, and there was little love lost between them and Edge.)

Sure enough, DX—Triple H and Shawn Michaels—came to the rescue. Edge was knocked back into the ring, practically into Cena's hands. An F-U, and it was all over. Cena had won.

The crowd loved it.

THE CROWD TURNS

One of the interesting facets of this showdown was the evolution of the crowd's reaction toward Cena. Starting as a very unpopular character, he ended his series with Edge to cheers. Partly, this was because of Edge's continued treachery and relentless turn toward the darker side of the wrestling arts. But fans were also impressed by the sheer amount of punishment Cena—as well as Edge—had endured during the campaign.

DX
VS. THE McMAHONS

If it's hard for a single wrestler to dominate the ring for very long, imagine how much more difficult it can be for a number of wrestlers. Over time even the most talented and famous tend to be weighed down and pulled apart. With only a handful of very notable exceptions—the Four Horsemen spring to mind—wrestling alliances haven't been able to both be successful and remain together for very long.

And once they fall apart, their story is over. No matter how magical the alliance was, the group's day has past, never to be revived.

But is that really the way it has to be? Can't a truly great alliance rise from the dead?

In fact, it can . . . as DX proved in its showdown with the McMahons.

FIRST TIME AROUND

D-Generation X debuted in World Wrestling Federation during the fall of 1997, during the height of the Monday Night

Wars. In many ways, they were an answer to WCW's New World Order. Young, energetic, and brash, DX rebelled against the powers-that-were at the head of World Wrestling Federation. They were heels, but in The Attitude Era of wrestling they helped usher in, they were *cool* heels and thus extremely popular pretty much from the start.

REBIRTH

Gone but not forgotten, DX was in some ways a slumbering giant, waiting for the right moment to be revived.

What would it take? A reconciliation between Michaels and Triple H, certainly, but something more—something from the fans, perhaps?

Crotch chops (fake karate chops in the groin area, the group's "salute") by Michaels and Triple H at *WrestleMania* 22 in 2006 drew big applause from the crowd, a sure sign that fans remembered the group with affection.

Within days, fans were clamoring for DX's revival. If Triple H and Michaels needed any more encouragement to revive the group, they had it now—in spades.

DX: THE REUNION

Both Michaels and Triple H had trouble with Mr. McMahon during the next few shows. Claiming that he was starting a new religion called McMahonism, Mr. McMahon in April declared that all the wrestlers would have to join in and worship him. Michaels came out and decked him.

Backstage, Triple H took a somewhat less aggressive approach, suggesting that Mr. McMahon drop the religious angle. McMahonism faded from the story line a few weeks afterward, but the trouble between Mr. McMahon and the two wrestlers remained strong.

At one point, Triple H hit Mr. McMahon's son Shane with a sledgehammer, ostensibly while aiming for Michaels, though it would soon become obvious that he had hit what he had truly been aiming at.

Mr. McMahon got his revenge against Michaels May 22 on *Raw* in a Five-on-One match with the Spirit Squad, a team of enforcers who did Mr. McMahon's bidding.

Triple H interfered at the end of the Michaels-Spirit match, preventing one of the Spirit Squad members from crippling Michaels. This set up more conflict between Mr. McMahon and Triple H, as McMahon arranged a match between Triple H and the Spirit Squad for the June 12 *Raw*.

To this point, Triple H and Shawn Michaels were operating as lone amigos. There may have been a bit of animosity leftover from their memorable Hell in a Cell match at *Bad Blood 2004*. But the DX reunion became official when Michaels came down and took out the Spirit Squad as they pummeled Triple H in a Five-on-One Gauntlet match.

Energized, the crowd rose to its feet as Triple H completed the rout. The two wrestlers put their foreheads together—literally—in the center of the ring. DX had been reborn.

A-MOCKING WE WILL GO

Mr. McMahon represented authority; DX had no respect for authority. Conflict was inevitable.

Mr. McMahon gave as good—or almost as good—as he got. In one memorable moment, Triple H mooned Mr. McMahon; Mr. McMahon lowered his drawers and invited DX to kiss his ass. The conflict ramped up.

On the June 26 *Raw*, Triple H dressed as if he were

Mr. McMahon, then went out on stage and claimed that he loved dicks—and then, of course, named people with the first name of Dick.

Michaels soon appeared, pretending to be Shane McMahon. He did a break-dancing thing (riffing on a '70s tape Shane had made) that left the audience . . . silent.

The real Mr. McMahon finally appeared, saying, "It's about time for this DX crap to come to an end."

Standing at the entrance tunnel to the arena, Mr. McMahon, (the real) Shane, and McMahon's Spirit Squad promised to beat the crap out of Michaels and Triple H.

The heavens—or rather a cargo net above the entrance—opened. Mr. McMahon and the others were showered with—to use Mr. McMahon's word—excrement.

NO RESPECT

"I've had enough," said Mr. McMahon the following week, after barring Triple H from the ring. "I've had enough."

He didn't say much more than that—his microphone had been sabotaged by DX.

The crowd shouted him down with a chant of "asshole."

The malfunctions continued, changing the pitch on his voice to something higher than Alvin and the Chipmunks.

"Damn it. You people think this is funny?" Mr. McMahon asked.

The crowd did indeed.

A loud fart cracked the audience up further. Mr. McMahon blamed DX, of course, saying they had no respect for him or the business.

Taking over the telecaster, one of the DX members (it appeared it was Michaels) drew a picture of a rooster, then wrote a dialogue balloon from Vince's mouth that pro-claimed, "I love cocks."

Crude and rude, but that was DX.

DOWN AND OUT

The showdown pushed toward a wrestling showdown be-tween DX and the Spirit Squad at *Saturday Night's Main Event* on July 15 in Texas.

Designed as a Handicap Elimination match, the contest called for a wrestler to be locked into a cage next to the ring once he was eliminated. Michaels and Triple H quickly ran the Spirit Squad from the ring—only to have Mr. McMahon unlock his supporters. Michaels cut their rally short, down-ing McMahon and locking him in the cage with the others.

Crotch chops on the top of the cage by DX completed the humiliation.

Mr. McMahon, naturally, wanted revenge. He set up a Tag Team match with DX for *SummerSlam* in August. This time, he was taking matters into his own hands: His son Shane would be his partner.

A BRIEF INTERLUDE

The feud continued unabated as the month went on. DX unveiled "Vince Loves Cock" T-shirts. The audience chanted the slogan.

The *SummerSlam* tag team battle, which went off just be-fore the main event, started with interference from the Spirit Squad. A number of *SmackDown!* and ECW wrestlers came down and softened up DX, leaving Triple H and Michaels laid out in and around the ring. One of the highlights of this part of the match was the brief but intense confrontation between Michaels and Big Show. Michaels at one point jumped on top of the ECW Champion, who took a few punches, then flicked him off like a fly.

Once the pummeling was over, the McMahons finally entered the ring. Michaels, barely conscious, took a beating for a few minutes, as the two men managed to throw the battered wrestler back and forth like a rag doll. Despite a chant from the crowd, Triple H lay flattened on the remains of the announcers' table.

The event featured a tribute to some of the franchise's old wrestlers, with the McMahons resurrecting old moves, including the Doomsday Device used by the Road Warriors and a Hart Attack (a lariat combination bear hug, perfected by The Hart Foundation). But old school couldn't save them.

Michaels managed a kickout on a two count, then took his opponents out with a double clothesline. Triple H finally made it back inside the ropes, and now it was his turn to put on an exhibition.

Triple H bodyslammed Mr. McMahon to the canvas, but interference by Umaga threatened to give the match to the McMahons. Kane came in and ran off Umaga . . . things were getting very confused as the McMahons revived and tried to steal a win. But DX rallied, and to the audience's delight, Mr. McMahon was counted out.

AT IT AGAIN

They'd lost, but the McMahons' credible performance in the ring stiffened their resolve, and they continued to mix it up with DX over the next few weeks.

After Triple H was knocked unconscious on a September

Raw, the showdown culminated in a Hell in a Cell match at *Unforgiven*, September 17, 2006. Big Show was once again in the McMahons' corner, this time playing a critical role in the match.

Big Show caught Shawn Michaels as he flew across the ring, evening the odds until DX managed to put him down. From that point, the McMahons caught holy hell, until Shane squashed a garbage can against a prone Triple H. Both DX members then took about ten minutes' worth of pounding, until Michaels and Triple H were barely able to stand. Mr. McMahon went to the middle of the ring and lowered his pants; he wanted Michaels to kiss his ass. But Triple H leveled him, and the momentum once more turned.

With Big Show down, DX began double-teaming Shane. Then it was Big Show's turn. Michaels and Triple H knocked him out, tied him into the ropes, and pulled down his pants.

Down on his knees, Mr. McMahon pleaded for mercy.

He didn't get it. Michaels and Triple H rammed his head into Big Show's ass.

And that's where the showdown ended.

UNDERTAKER VS. BATISTA

There's nothing like a showdown between too very large men, especially when they are both at the top of their game. The Undertaker-Batista face-off played out in the early part of 2007 was exactly that sort of confrontation. Fans were thrilled by the big men's athleticism, not something most expect when the combatants are pushing three hundred pounds.

RAW CHOKESLAM

While Undertaker had held several championship belts during his long career, he had never been the World Heavyweight Champion. So his decision to take on Batista, made during a February 2007 *Raw* episode, shouldn't have been surprising.

What *was* surprising was the way he did it. Facing all three of WWE's champions, he walked over to Batista, picked him up by the neck, and chokeslammed him to the ground.

While they were not friends, they had both been shrugging off the same nemesis: Mr. Kennedy, who was making a habit of pissing off audiences by taking on their favorites. And Undertaker and Batista were also scheduled to work together as a tag team against Shawn Michaels and John Cena at *No Way Out*, the February Pay-Per-View.

Undertaker's chokeslam clearly bothered Batista, though he claimed the opposite. He had only recently returned to take the title, fighting his way back from injuries a few months before. While he said he feared no man and no wrestler, he still seemed somewhat nervous on camera when interviewed in the weeks going into the fight.

Undertaker had never lost at *WrestleMania*, and for all his talk about how much his respect for the man wouldn't interfere with his wrestling, Batista had to be at least a little concerned about how he was going to break that streak.

TURNCOAT

Undertaker had caught Batista off guard at *Raw* with his chokeslam. When the pair met Michaels and Cena as a tag team, Batista got a chance to turn the tables.

If size alone determined the outcome of a wrestling match, Cena and Michaels would have been outclassed from the start. As it was, they were overshadowed by the bigger pair for much of the match. At one point, Undertaker simply boosted Michaels into the air, held him there for a few seconds, then tossed him like a piece of paper out of the ring. Undertaker and Batista took turns pummeling their opponents, each trying to outdo the other—perhaps as a show of what they would do to each other at *WrestleMania*.

After a long beating, Michaels managed to reach the ropes, bringing a fresh Cena into the fray. Cena dominated both men in succession, until a four-way Free-For-All developed. Once again, Undertaker and Batista used their superior size to full advantage.

It looked like the pair were going to go into their showdown at *WrestleMania* as friends and allies. But as Undertaker prepared to pin the dazed Cena, Batista suddenly grabbed the Dead Man and threw him to the canvas. Undertaker was stunned—and so was the crowd.

Batista stood back and watched as Michaels and Cena ganged up on his dazed partner, pinning him in seconds.

Payback wasn't a bitch, it was a Batista.

WRESTLEMANIA 23

While Undertaker was a favorite going into *WrestleMania* at Ford Field in Detroit, Batista had his share of partisans. Many believed that if Undertaker's *WrestleMania* string was to be broken before he retired—another rumor that made the rounds in 2007—Batista would be the one to do it.

Batista entered the arena, doing his patented fireworks-enhanced break dance. Undertaker, dressed as a cross between a Western gunfighter and a resurrected ghoul, floated in after him.

An exchange of glares, and the match was on.

Batista landed the first blow, driving into Undertaker's midsection and taking him to the canvas. He unleashed a fury of punches, gaining the early momentum and holding it into the middle of the match. Batista wrestled as if he were a good fifty pounds lighter, flying off the top rope, exploding with a clothesline, and even bodyslamming the (slightly) bigger Undertaker flat to the mat.

Before five minutes had passed, a good portion of the

audience was holding its breath, certain that Undertaker was about to lose.

They didn't want to see that. In fact, every time a punch by Batista landed during one stretch, the crowd booed. Every blow by Undertaker brought loud applause.

Undertaker, beginning to turn the tide, showed off some athleticism of his own, diving out of the ring at Batista with a flying move over the ropes. He bounced his opponent off the barricade, dazing him, and it looked as if Undertaker would drag Batista back into the ring for the pin and the title.

As so often in wrestling, the tide turned yet again; Batista came back to life, throwing Undertaker through the bell table in the process.

At this point, Batista could have won the match by returning to the ring and staying long enough for Undertaker to be disqualified. (Unlike Undertaker, he could hold on to the title if the match ended in a disqualification.) But he had guaranteed a pin, and that's what he wanted.

Actually, he seemed to want more than that, chasing Undertaker beneath a table for a fresh thrashing. The two wrestlers dismantled the announcers' section as Batista put Undertaker through yet another table with a running power-slam.

Back in the ring, Batista couldn't force a pin, his prey slipping away a half tick before three several times. Finally, Undertaker got his wind. They exchanged some of the their best moves, both narrowly escaping pins.

Batista managed a Batista bomb—his finishing move. Undertaker kicked out, the first victim to ever do so.

Surprised and exhausted, Batista left himself open for a piledriver—and the championship changed hands.

REMATCH

The back-and-forth nature of the final minutes, as well as the energy the two large men showed, convinced many fans to rate the match the best of *WrestleMania 23*, even though it was not the featured contest.

The audience reaction as well as the outcome suggested a rematch, and Batista was quick to demand one at the next *SmackDown!* aired later that week.

The rematch was booked as a Last-Man-Standing at *Backlash*, held in Atlanta. The format calls for a win by knockout rather than pin: If a wrestler can't get to his feet by a count of ten, he loses. Classically, these hard-core showdowns are brutal affairs, slugging contests as much as wrestling matches.

Batista had injured a hamstring weeks earlier and had his leg wrapped as he entered the ring. He was reported to be in tremendous pain the morning of the match, though it was impossible to tell from his performance.

The early going was almost the mirror image of their *WrestleMania* bout, with Undertaker holding the upper hand as he took the match to Batista. With the action moving outside of the ring, Undertaker zeroed in on his leg.

Batista, limping and heavily favoring his injury, managed to rebound, knocking Undertaker down twice for long counts. Husbanding his energy into sudden bursts, Batista waged war outside the ring, with the match once more playing as an inverse of the *WrestleMania* showdown. Undertaker smacked him with the steel steps; blood began running from Batista's forehead. After Batista collapsed onto one of the tables, Undertaker leaped onto him. The combined six hundred pounds was too much for the table, which squished under them.

Batista beat a ten count—much of the audience, once more favoring Undertaker, booed—and went back for more. Rallying, he put Undertaker down for several knockdowns. The crowd began to waver—there were cheers after a quick pair of spinebusters laid Undertaker down for a nine count. More action—more reverse parallels to the *WrestleMania* showdown—left Batista so frustrated he grabbed a steel chair from the audience and slapped Undertaker across the skull (a legal shot under the rules of the match).

Another series of near knockdowns by both wrestlers ensued. Kicked from the ring, Batista staggered backward under the slow onslaught of an exhausted Undertaker, who pushed him back toward the entrance area.

The wrestlers' fatigue became the focus of the contest as the two men seemed to launch their punches and moves against each other in slow motion. The fight recalled contests held before most of the audience had even been born, the old days of wrestling where endurance was more important than style.

When they reached the entrance stage, both men erupted with a fury of punches. Finally finding his strength, Batista threw everything into a spear that carried Undertaker off the stage and into a light pole, which collapsed on top of both men.

The match was over, without a clear winner.

INTERRUPTED

It had been an epic struggle, but it ended prematurely.

The showdown next headed to a Cage match on *Smack-Down!* in Birmingham, Alabama, on May 4.

Undertaker had injured his arm, and it showed. Still, after

more than fifteen minutes, he managed to drop himself out of the cage at the same time as Batista, retaining the championship.

But.

But.

Mark Henry—the World's Strongest Man, who had vowed to make his mark as a presence on *SmackDown!*—ran in and bashed the depleted Undertaker, leaving him senseless in the middle of the ring.

Edge, who'd won a Money-in-the-Bank title shot earlier, immediately cashed in and had an easy time taking the title off the comatose Dead Man. Edge went on to feud with Batista and others; Undertaker was out of action as he recuperated from the bashings Batista had inflicted.

BACK AT IT

Undertaker returned at September 2007's *Unforgiven* and was soon pursuing the championship belt once more. Batista had won the championship belt back in a three-way contest with Rey Mysterio and Khali at the same Pay-Per-View. They clashed in a World Title match at *Cyber Sunday* in October. The referee, chosen by the fans, was Stone Cold Steve Austin.

The match began with Batista running across the stage at his opponent, and the early third of the fight was mostly an exhibit of Batista's various punching techniques. Undertaker reversed the momentum in the middle third of the match, and for a while it looked like it would end early. But with Undertaker dominating, a throw by Batista brought the crowd to its feet.

A charge into the ring post damaged Batista's shoulder,

but he had enough left to catch Undertaker when he leaped from the top rope—one of the few times the Dead Man was unable to put his opponent down with the move. Batista slammed Undertaker to the mat, stunning him with a spinebuster.

Undertaker rebounded with a triangle choke (a leghold that cuts off oxygen to the brain). Fighting for his breath, his consciousness, and his title, Batista struggled to his knees and forced Undertaker's shoulders back against the canvas, just missing a pin but winning a release from the hold.

Undertaker raised Batista above his head with a chokeslam, then found himself speared and taken down to the canvas.

At *WrestleMania*, the crowd had been lopsided in favoring Undertaker. But now, the fans seemed much more evenly split. The audience counted out for both men as they narrowly missed pins. They threw each other around with abandon, and it was all Stone Cold could do to stay out of the way. After Undertaker kicked out of a pin following a Batista bomb, the Animal reached back and with the roar of the crowd behind him, dropped Undertaker with another bomb, then grabbed his leg and held on for the pin.

ONE MORE TIME

Batista had been practically begging for a Hell in a Cell match, and he finally got his wish at *Survivor Series* November 18, 2007.

Undertaker dominated the first eight or nine minutes of the contest, at one point grating Batista's face across the links of the fence. A vintage apron slam left Batista so dazed that Undertaker was able to give him a reverse chair slam to the throat, smashing him against a chair top as he slammed the chair against the stairs (a legal hit under the rules of the match). It was a vicious cycle of punishment.

But it wasn't enough to win.

A desperate spinebuster by Batista stopped the onslaught—temporarily.

Soon Undertaker was back to launching Batista into the fence. Batista was cut badly and began to bleed.

Escaping a triangle choke by grabbing the rope, Batista began a comeback that saw him bash Undertaker's skull with the steel steps. Now it was Undertaker's turn to bleed. The audience counted Batista's blows as he laid into Undertaker on the turnbuckle.

Turnaround was common in this series, and soon Undertaker was back on top, with Batista staggering around as if punch-drunk. A few shots later, it was Undertaker who was staggered.

Batista hopped out of the ring and fished out a table from below. Setting it up, he launched Undertaker through the top.

Somehow, Undertaker avoided the pin.

Minutes later, after an Undertaker Tombstone, Batista did the same, kicking out at the last possible moment.

Exhausted, both men fought on. Undertaker finally managed to piledrive Batista into the stairs that had been left in the middle of the ring. Undertaker was able to cover—barely—and looked like he was going to get the pin. But when the ref reached two, Batista was pulled out of the ring by Edge, who had gotten inside the cage by posing as a cameraman. Using the camera to lay out Undertaker, he hauled Batista over to Undertaker, preserving the championship.

But for whom?

He thought he was doing it for himself, but now Edge was in the mix, and he wasn't about to go quietly.

PSYCHO

Edge's run-in started a three-way conflict that culminated in a Triple-Threat match with Batista and Undertaker at *Armageddon* in December. There, Edge regained the crown and some standing as one of the top Superstars. There were actually three Edges in the match, making it a five-way . . . but that's another story.

The Batista-Undertaker showdowns were notable for the gargantuan physical effort put out by the two big men. As each match drove to its conclusion, the audience felt their exhaustion. Allegiances shifted not just with every match but seemingly with every blow.

As they should, in all great showdowns.